Nancy Copley

GORGAS HOME
CAMPUS - UNIVERSITY OF ALABAMA
FAMOUS TUSCALOOSA LANDMARKS

AMELIA GAYLE GORGAS

AMELIA GAYLE GORGAS

A BIOGRAPHY

by

MARY TABB JOHNSTON

with

ELIZABETH JOHNSTON LIPSCOMB

THE UNIVERSITY OF ALABAMA PRESS
University, Alabama

The quotation on page 118 is from
WILLIAM CRAWFORD GORGAS, HIS LIFE AND WORK
by Marie D. Gorgas and Burton J. Hendrick.
Copyright © 1924 by Doubleday & Company, Inc.
Reprinted by permission of the Publisher.

Library of Congress Cataloging in Publication Data

Johnston, Mary Tabb.
  Amelia Gayle Gorgas: a biography.

  1. Gorgas, Amelia Gayle. 2. College librar-
ians—Alabama—Biography. 3. Alabama. University.
Library—Biography. I. Lipscomb, Elizabeth
Johnston.

Z720.G67J64   027.7′ 092′4 [B]   77–18889
ISBN 0-8173-5235-X

CONTENTS

FAMILY OF
AMELIA GAYLE GORGAS

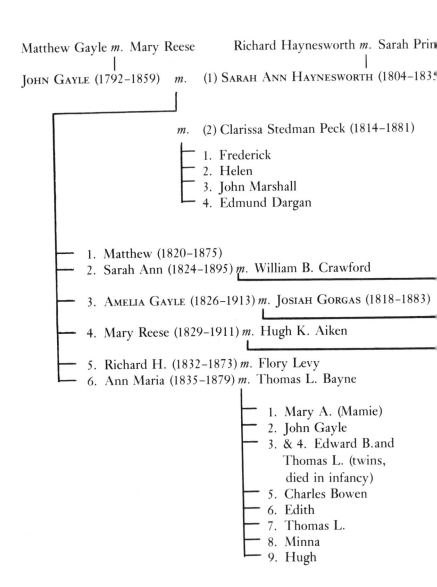

Matthew Gayle *m.* Mary Reese   Richard Haynesworth *m.* Sarah Prin

JOHN GAYLE (1792–1859)   *m.*   (1) SARAH ANN HAYNESWORTH (1804–183!

m.   (2) Clarissa Stedman Peck (1814–1881)

1. Frederick
2. Helen
3. John Marshall
4. Edmund Dargan

1. Matthew (1820–1875)
2. Sarah Ann (1824–1895) *m.* William B. Crawford

3. AMELIA GAYLE (1826–1913) *m.* JOSIAH GORGAS (1818–1883)

4. Mary Reese (1829–1911) *m.* Hugh K. Aiken

5. Richard H. (1832–1873) *m.* Flory Levy
6. Ann Maria (1835–1879) *m.* Thomas L. Bayne

1. Mary A. (Mamie)
2. John Gayle
3. & 4. Edward B. and
   Thomas L. (twins,
   died in infancy)
5. Charles Bowen
6. Edith
7. Thomas L.
8. Minna
9. Hugh

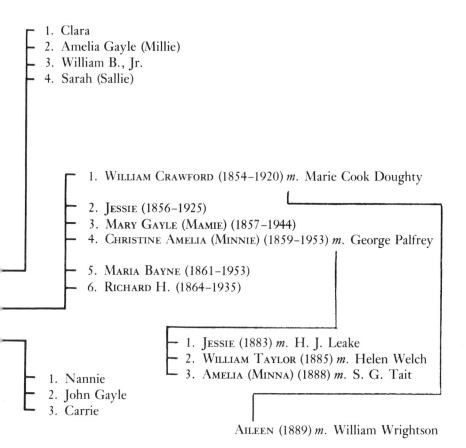

1. Clara
2. Amelia Gayle (Millie)
3. William B., Jr.
4. Sarah (Sallie)

1. WILLIAM CRAWFORD (1854–1920) *m.* Marie Cook Doughty
2. JESSIE (1856–1925)
3. MARY GAYLE (MAMIE) (1857–1944)
4. CHRISTINE AMELIA (MINNIE) (1859–1953) *m.* George Palfrey
5. MARIA BAYNE (1861–1953)
6. RICHARD H. (1864–1935)

1. JESSIE (1883) *m.* H. J. Leake
2. WILLIAM TAYLOR (1885) *m.* Helen Welch
3. AMELIA (MINNA) (1888) *m.* S. G. Tait

1. Nannie
2. John Gayle
3. Carrie

AILEEN (1889) *m.* William Wrightson

FOR ANNE TAYLOR

PREFACE

In going through the family papers following the death of Amelia Gayle Gorgas, her children and grandchildren found themselves the possessors of a vast number of letters and documents containing an abundance of social, political, and family history. Through the years they made this material available to scholars. Biographies of General Josiah Gorgas and of General William Crawford Gorgas were written and published. As early as 1948 the two then-surviving daughters of Mrs. Gorgas expressed the desire that a biography of their mother might be written, and they urged Dr. Anne Gary Pannell, at that time a member of the history faculty of The University of Alabama, to undertake the task. Because of unforeseen circumstances and the pressure of administrative duties after she became president of Sweet Briar College, Dr. Pannell was unable to begin the writing of the book, though with a grant from the Research Committee of The University of Alabama she had done some preliminary work on the Gorgas papers. These papers were given to The University of Alabama by Mrs. Gorgas's granddaughters, Mrs. Jessie Palfrey Leake and Mrs. S. G. Tait, in March 1958 and became known as the Gayle-Gorgas Collection.

In 1967 I volunteered to undertake some of the research for Dr. Pannell and was soon so thoroughly engrossed in the study that when Dr. Pannell (now Mrs. George A. Taylor) expressed a willingness for me to carry the project through to its conclusion, I was delighted. It has been a task that has given me great joy. Mrs. Leake and Mrs. Tait encouraged me as no one else could have and were generous in finding additional material that had not been given to the University. Mrs. Tait's son, Mr. George Tait, and his wife made even more material available and allowed me to use their copies of some of the original papers in the library of The University of Alabama, which enabled me more easily to carry on the work at my home in Virginia. I am deeply indebted to them and to Miss Mary Adams Hughes of Edgefield, South Carolina, a great-niece of Amelia Gayle Gorgas. She lent me the journals, scrapbooks, and letters of her grandmother, Sarah Gayle Crawford, all of which were a tremendous help in writing of the years before Amelia Gayle was married. Miss Mary Gayle Robertson of Columbia, South Carolina, another great-niece, was very gracious to me, and I was able to use some of her family papers in the Gayle-Aiken Collection of the South Caroliniana Library of the University of South Carolina.

I wish to express my deep appreciation to Dr. W. Stanley Hoole, former librarian of The University of Alabama, who shared his thorough knowledge of the material in the Gayle-Gorgas Collection with me and encouraged me by his interest in my undertaking. Mrs. Frances Barton of the William Stanley Hoole Special Collections Library of the Amelia Gayle Gorgas Library, The University of Alabama never seemed too busy to search for material or to send photocopies to me in Virginia when needed. To her also I express my sincere thanks.

I am grateful to the staff of the Southern Historical Collection at the University of North Carolina at Chapel Hill; to those who assisted me in the Mobile Public Library, at the South Caroliniana Library in Columbia, South Carolina, and in the Manuscript Division of the Library of Congress; and to Mr. Milo B. Howard, Jr., and Mrs. Clara Kennedy Jones of the Alabama State Department of Archives and History in Montgomery, Alabama. The archives of the Jessie Ball duPont Library of the University of the South at Sewanee, Tennessee, also provided help, as did the Virginia State Library, the Virginia Historical Society Library, the New York Public Library, and Mrs. Clara F. Clapp of the Carnegie Foundation for the Advancement of Teaching. I have used the facilities of the C. M. Newman Library of the Virginia Polytechnic Institute and State University frequently and wish to acknowledge my indebtedness to its staff.

I owe an especial debt of gratitude to Professor Frank Vandiver, provost of Rice University, whose biography of Josiah Gorgas, *Ploughshares into Swords*, was invaluable. I am also indebted to John Mendinghall Gibson for his biography of William Crawford Gorgas, *Physician to the World*.

My husband, George Burke Johnston, whose personal library of Alabama history and biography has been very helpful, has encouraged me every step of the way. In a reversal of the usual roles he has done a great deal of the typing. My daughter Elizabeth Johnston Lipscomb edited the manuscript and is responsible in large measure for its final form.

Blacksburg, Virginia   Mary Tabb Lancaster Johnston
May 19, 1977

INTRODUCTION

Amelia Gayle Gorgas is most easily identified as the daughter of John Gayle, governor of Alabama from 1831 to 1835, the wife of General Josiah Gorgas, head of the Confederate Ordnance Department, and the mother of General William Crawford Gorgas, who won international acclaim for his work in conquering yellow fever in Cuba and the Panama Canal Zone. Yet she is of interest to the contemporary reader not only for the reflected glory of the men in her life but also for her own accomplishments. She was widely recognized throughout her native state for her influence on the students of The University of Alabama during the years she served as librarian there. Her services brought her a pension from the Carnegie Foundation, the second such grant ever given to a woman, and the University library was named for her. In 1977 Amelia Gayle Gorgas was elected to the Alabama Women's Hall of Fame.

Mrs. Gorgas's work at The University of Alabama, which occupied her from her fifty-fifth to eighty-first year, was the culmination of a remarkable life. This life was notable not so much for drama and crisis—though she lived in dramatic times—as for the strength, flexibility, and resiliency that characterized so many of the purportedly fragile, helpless Southern women of her generation. She adapted herself readily to the relative prosperity of her early married life as wife of a United States Army officer in Maine, the tensions and dangers of Richmond during the Civil War, the struggle to make a new life in the economically depressed South in the period immediately after the war, and the pleasures and problems of the academic communities in Sewanee and Tuscaloosa.

Her early letters reveal many of the characteristics that enabled her to deal successfully with the variety of roles she was called on to play later in her life: her gift for caring for children and the sick, her intellectual curiosity, which made her a well-educated woman in spite of little formal education by modern standards, and her ability to charm all those around her, from senators to school boys. The same qualities that made her a favorite of her friends' children and a devoted mother later made her a sympathetic counselor and confidante to the boys in her charge at Sewanee and The University of Alabama.

The center of her life was always her family, and in her relationships with her husband and their six children her strengths are most fully revealed. Her happy and fulfilling marriage was not one between a domineering man and a submissive woman but a partnership in which each depended on the other for advice and support. She and Josiah shared their concerns about their children, their health, finances, and politics; and Amelia was as capable of handling business arrangements at their Brierfield ironworks during her husband's absences as she was of altering the children's winter clothes to save the expense of new ones in the hard years after the war.

Although her life seems in many ways "liberated," she was not a feminist. Her attitude perhaps reflects that of many women of her age and class who had to be competent managers to provide for their large families and yet at the same time enjoyed occupying the pedestals provided for them by popular sentiment.

The life of Amelia Gayle Gorgas holds a double fascination for twentieth-century readers. It is both the record of an attractive and appealing individual in her particular circumstances and the account of a sizeable segment of nineteenth-century American society.

ELIZABETH JOHNSTON LIPSCOMB

AMELIA GAYLE GORGAS

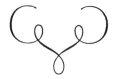

1

A MOTHER'S
HOPES AND FEARS

IN THE YEAR 1826 the town of Greensboro, Alabama, was ten years old. The fertile area about 150 miles north of Mobile was settled in 1816 by pioneers from North and South Carolina, Georgia, Tennessee, and Kentucky, and the town grew rapidly. Mail delivery began in 1818, letters being carried fifty miles on horseback from Cahaba, Alabama's first capital. By 1822 the community boasted a hotel, five stores, and a law office, and in 1823 the Alabama legislature granted a charter for the incorporation of the "Town of Greensborough in the county of Greene."[1]

Into this thriving community in the spring of 1826 John Gayle, judge of the Third Judicial Circuit of Alabama, brought his wife, Sarah Ann Haynesworth Gayle, and their two children, Matthew and Sarah, to make their home. Their third child, Amelia Ross Gayle, was born in Greensboro on June 1, 1826.[2] She was named for her mother's girlhood friend, Amelia Fisher Ross.

Born in Sumter County, South Carolina, both John and Sarah Gayle had been raised in south Alabama where their families had become close friends. John had returned to his native state for his college education, graduating in 1813 from South Carolina College, a well-known training ground for politicians. He then read law with Judge Abner S. Lipscomb at St. Stephens, Alabama, and set up a practice at Claiborne in Monroe County in 1818. He married Sarah Haynesworth, a charming brunette twelve years his junior, in the following year, a few months before her sixteenth birthday.

John Gayle's political career began in 1822 with his election to the state legislature as a representative of Monroe County. A year later he was elected judge. His new position required him to hold at least two sessions of the court annually in each of the counties in his district,[3] and because his circuit embraced several of the most populous areas of the state, he often had to be away from home for long periods of time. With a desire to be as centrally located as possible he decided to settle in Greensboro, just thirty-five miles from Tuscaloosa, the new state capital.

While John Gayle carried out his judicial responsibilities during the weeks following Amelia's birth, Sarah and the children began to feel at home in Greensboro. Thomas Eastin, who had married John Gayle's sister, Lucinda, edited the Greensboro *Halcyon*, and Levin Gayle, John's brother, had business interests in the town. Members of the three families kept in close touch. Sarah had brought from her old home several family servants, among them Hampton and his wife Hetty. Their labors left her with leisure for calling on new friends, reading, and writing verses for her friends' albums. She also enjoyed attending religious services held by the Methodists, Baptists, and Presbyterians who had established congregations in the early days of the community.[4] Sarah found time to keep a journal that was a combination of moral reflections, flights of sentiment, and local gossip. She frequently recorded her impressions of the children's progress, noting in the autumn of 1827 that Amelia "runs over the yard now, a dark bright-eyed, lively intelligent child."

Resigning his judgeship in 1828, John Gayle began to practice law in Greensboro. His presence at home was needed, for Sarah was in poor health and found his long absences "terrible." In addition, work was progressing on their new home, and his supervision was necessary. Built on the south side of the town's main street, the large brick house had an adjoining kitchen and smokehouse. On March 5 Sarah had written that "our house goes on now and begins to look handsome."[5] When he came home to stay, the judge was almost a stranger to young Amelia, but Sarah recorded that the "attentive gentleness he knows how to show children and which is indeed natural to him, served to reconcile her to him and by the time we retired for the night her little curly head was laid upon his bosom."[6]

John Gayle was not to stay long out of politics. He was again persuaded to run for the legislature and in August 1829 was elected to represent Greene County. When he went to Tuscaloosa for the fall session, he was chosen Speaker of the House. Two years later he was elected governor of Alabama, the candidate of the Democrats, who were for the most part supporters of Andrew Jackson.[7]

Governor Gayle hoped to move his family, which now included a third daughter, Mary Reese, to Tuscaloosa with him, but by the time of his inauguration his wife was again pregnant and said that she could not make the move for at least a year. In December of that same year Gayle wrote to Sarah, offering to have her brought to Tuscaloosa for a visit, but she declined, saying that if he were sick she would not hesitate to come but her situation was not "propitious to visiting for mere amusement." A month later she wrote, "I begin to count the weeks and days which are to creep away before you come home," and soon afterward she pleaded, "Oh! Come home, for mercy's sake, what can a woman do without her husband?"[8] Meanwhile, Sarah often sent her husband requests for household items and books that he could secure in the state capital: "Matt says he wants one that tells of unknown Polar regions, not perceiving poor fellow, that he has made a bull of the expression—voyages and travels will answer at present. In addition get 'Conversations on Natural Philosophy,' Philip Massinger's plays, and if there is a vol. containing familiar descriptions of the wonderful things of this earth, put that in too."[9]

In Greensboro on February 26, 1832, Richard Haynesworth Gayle, named for his maternal grandfather, was born. That spring his mother, who was not regaining her strength as she had expected, wrote in a despondent mood of her fear for her children if she were to die, "Their father is all kindness but he is least calculated to chide or correct." It disturbed her that the children were destitute of maternal connections and that their father's relatives all had large families of their own and were in moderate circumstances. She worried particularly about little Amelia that summer, writing that she looked pale and thin with but little appetite. "Heaven bless her," she wrote, "she is the most affectionate docile child I have."

Plans to move to Tuscaloosa that autumn did not materialize, but on January 13, 1833, Sarah wrote in her journal:

> A hurried letter from Mr. Gayle informs me that we are to remove to Tuscaloosa immediately, the Legislature having at last required it,

and added the pitiful sum of $500 to defray some necessary expenses, growing out of a removal. It is half in joy, half in sorrow, that I prepare to take this step. My pleasure is great that we will at last be settled, be *at home*, for I cannot call that place home which I anticipate leaving every year. I love one, where I have planted my attachments with every climbing vine. . . .[10]

The move to Tuscaloosa took place in March. Because Alabama provided no residence for its chief executive, the Gayles took rooms at Ewing's Tavern on Broad Street,[11] a few blocks north of the new capitol. Sarah, whose talents and accomplishments made her much admired, performed her new duties as the governor's wife with dignity and grace. Mrs. Alva Woods, wife of the president of the University of Alabama, soon became one of her closest friends.

Sarah Gayle described many details of her life in Tuscaloosa in a voluminous correspondence with her friend, Mrs. Mary Peck of Greensboro. She sent lively accounts of family outings.

> Then what enchanting walks are on the river bank—elevated, retired and shaded. We went out this morning, our little troop composed of Amelia, Mary and Mary Ann [the nurse] with Dick, Mr. G. and myself. On we scrambled over "bank and over brae," until we stood on the bank. I found fishing rods, everything but the bait, which I insisted on an old log's furnishing—in another moment the line was cast, and I drew up—nothing! Then a boat was discovered, & at the peril of sliding into the water, I took possession; but most unluckily the hard hearted owner had provided against accidents by chaining it to a tree. But the chain was long, and I proved its length. I was delighted to find the power of managing the canoe return as soon as I took the paddle in my hands—I could have taken myself across, I think. Mr. Gayle sat upon the bank, playing with the children, who were wild with pleasure, . . .

On another occasion she wrote: "I do not know how it happens, but start to which church I will, I find myself at the Methodist, when I stop. I love the Methodist preaching, when it is quiet and reasonable. But I confess, I take a seat near the door, that, when some weak minded or hypocritical brother or sister of either color begins to rave, and stamp and shout, I may leave the place as I always do, without scruple, for when that begins, the good is ended with me . . .

we never heard of Christ or his immediate followers shouting, or encouraging it, and tho' Peter *wept* it was a silent *look*, which caused him to do so."

When Amelia was almost seven, she rode an Indian pony, which her father had purchased for the children, into the halls of the capitol itself prompting her mother to write Mrs. Peck, "Amelia is becoming wretchedly wild and I shall have to bring her to track immediately."[12] Gone, apparently, was the docile Amelia of the summer before.

In August 1833 John Gayle was reelected governor. One of his major concerns at this time was a potentially explosive conflict between the federal government and Alabama over the removal of white settlers from Creek Indian lands. In December of that year Francis Scott Key, then district attorney for the District of Columbia, was sent to mediate the controversy. Sarah Gayle recorded her impressions of his visit in her journal:

> Mr. Key, the Agent of the Government in this State, interests me greatly. He is a man of much intelligence, a lawyer of high standing—a man of honor—a poet—and a *Christian*. . . . He has been around frequently and sat an hour or two last night chatting to myself and the children. He made Sarah read for him, and then he read for her, some of the fine hymns and psalms in the book of common prayer, one of his own beginning with "Lord with glowing heart, I'd praise thee" in it. He seems to be fervently pious, and dearly do I love · to hear him talk on the subject. . . . [13]

Key wrote some verses in young Sarah's album, and Mrs. Gayle addressed a poem to him requesting that he also write in the album of a young friend, Margaret Kornegay, the niece of Alabama Senator William R. King.

The following February the Gayles moved to Medlock's Tavern, also conveniently near the capitol. When she made the move Sarah expressed concern for the childless innkeeper's wife at having the Gayles' five "wild ones" turned loose on the premises.[14] Boarding with so large a family gave rise to many problems: Mrs. Medlock complained of their servants; expenses were high, so the Gayles often worried over finances. They talked of selling their carriage and horses and hoped to find a buyer for their Greensboro house, in which the governor's chronically unemployed brother Levin and his family were now living.

All of the Gayles were saddened when Rose, the children's nurse, died of tetanus in April. Sarah wrote Mrs. Peck:

> She was ill nearly three weeks, and I am glad every day that I nursed her more like a child than a servant, all that time we had to move her off the Tavern lot on account of noise and I occupied a bed in her room at night, and was with her all day. She liked my nursing best, and she had it to the best of my ability.... No candle could have expired more gently. Death had no terrors, mental or bodily, no struggle withdrew her hand from her Master's, nor moved mine from her cold brow; and tho' my tears fell in torrents, it was because the spirit of my children's play-fellow and nurse was passing. Color makes a wide distinction in life, but in the hour of death there is not the slightest. As fervent a prayer rose up in my heart that at Judgment day we might all meet Rose again in happiness, as if she had been white as snow. The whole family, Mr. Gayle not excepted, as well as Mrs. Eastin's children, went with her to the grave and when the earth fell on her coffin, there was as sincere a grief as ever was, tho' perhaps differing in degree.

Mrs. Gayle wrote at the same time that she hoped to go down to the country for a visit, but she continued, "These plans of mine always fail, in consequence of the number of children to leave or take, one of which is as hard to do as the other."[15]

Several weeks later Sarah Gayle commented in her journal on Amelia's development: "I was pleased this morning to see evidence of sensibility in Amelia who was reading one of those simple but often affecting sunday school biographies placed in the hands of the children of our day. She did not know that anyone was observing her nor did I make any remark to her." On June 1, 1834, Sarah Gayle characterized her daughter prophetically:

> This is Amelia's birthday—she is eight years old. May a good and great God shower his blessings upon her, and lead her into "green pastures, where are living waters," by his own appointed path, much of good is in her character, much that may grow into evil. Constant care is requisite to manage her, and her animal spirits have constantly to be repressed. She is very affectionate and warm hearted—very

frank, often just, she is not at all indolent and learns readily. Easily led into temptation, it is necessary to keep her from mischievous and headlong company for she follows their lead. But she will be an estimable woman if rightly taught which must be done.[16]

Amelia's temperament was quite different from that of her older sister Sarah. Their mother noted that after her return from an absence: "Sarah walked almost slowly and awkwardly from the conscious feeling of joy, her cheeks flushed & the tears in her eyes. When I kissed her she hid her face. Amelia, on the contrary, seemed wild with unrestrained joy. Her cheeks, too, were crimsoned & she flew over the path throwing herself into my arms with every demonstration of delight."[17]

The Gayles spent a month in Greene County in the late summer of 1834 and arranged for the sale of their Greensboro home and the carriage and horses. By the end of the year plans were being made to move from Medlock's Tavern to a rented house about half a mile north of the capitol on the heights above the Black Warrior River. Though it would have been easier to stay at the inn for the few remaining months of John Gayle's term of office, Sarah looked forward to keeping house again "even in my imperfect way,"[18] and in the new home Ann Maria Gayle was born on February 19, 1835.

Governor Gayle planned to move his family to Mobile and return to the practice of law at the end of his term as governor, south Alabama offering a number of inducements. In going there they would in a sense be going home. Many friends and relatives had settled in Mobile, now Alabama's largest city with a population of about 10,000. A contemporary, the famous actor Tyrone Power, who visited Mobile in 1835, observed: "This little city was to me one of the most attractive spots I visited south of the Potomac. . . . I found here . . . the best conducted and best appointed hotel in the Southern Country, and society congenial and amiable. . . . "[19]

Young Sarah Ann Gayle was sent on a visit to her prospective home early in 1835, armed with a list of friends she was to see and numerous instructions from her mother: "Give as little trouble as possible to those with whom you are staying. Be modest in conversation & conduct tho' I hope this is an unnecessary charge . . . attend to your album . . . In short, do what is right, shun what is wrong—keep your eyes and ears open, and your mouth shut, most of the time. Practice your music every chance. Be clean and neat. Keep a journal—write to me every two or three days...."[20]

In late June state business took Governor Gayle to north Alabama. In a letter headed "Glorious 4, 1835," his wife wrote:

I am doubtful if a letter has the least chance to find you, leading such a wandering life as you are now, yet I hope this may, that you may know Gen'l Parsons is out for your successor. This was announced in forum today at the Methodist Church . . . and I suppose I heard what may be called a stump speech. It was excellently well received, and amused me exceedingly, tho' when he began, and I looked at John Gayle's possible successor I thought I should have screamed as Fanny Kemble has it. By the way, she is a famous piece, and in spite of some most pinching truths, I like her book. You have no idea what delightful touches of warm, natural feeling are in it, and what is more, I find some of my own embodied, and fixed off with drapery that my poor vocabulary could never furnish.[21]

She added that the general had declared himself a Jackson man and that she had her own thoughts about the enthusiastic manner in which the candidate had been received. John Gayle's own feelings toward Jackson had cooled considerably since the conflict between the state and the national governments over the Indian lands.

This letter was one of Sarah's last. Later in the month she developed tetanus following some dental work, and on July 30, 1835, she died. Up until the end she hoped for the return of her husband, but word of her illness failed to reach him in time. With a last effort she wrote on a scrap of paper, "I testify with my dying breath that since first I laid my young heart upon his manly bosom I have known only love and happiness."[22] Funeral services were announced for Friday, July 31st, 1835:

The friends and acquaintances of Mrs. Sarah A. Gayle are requested to attend her funeral, this afternoon at the hour of four o'clock, from the residence of Gov. Gayle to the Methodist Church where Divine Service will be performed and from thence to the place of interment.

Sarah Ann Haynesworth Gayle left behind her six young children, ranging in age from fourteen-year-old Matt, a student at the

University of Alabama, to five-month-old Maria. The governor received offers of help from a number of friends and relatives. When he moved to Mobile in the autumn, Mary and Richard were placed in the care of his cousin Billups Gayle and his wife, while baby Maria remained the chief concern of Hetty, the family servant who had accompanied the Gayles to Tuscaloosa and was taken to Mobile by the widowed governor. Matt continued his work at the University while boarding at the home of Henry Tutwiler, professor of ancient languages. Sarah entered boarding school in Tuscaloosa, and nine-year-old Amelia went to live with her mother's dear friend Mrs. Alva Woods.[23]

A HOME IN MOBILE

AMELIA WAS TO REMAIN for more than two years in her new home on the University of Alabama campus where the Woods lived with their ten-year-old son, Marshall. The University was situated on about eighty acres of land north of Tuscaloosa on what was then called the Huntsville Road. The architect, Captain William Nicholls, had modeled the first buildings somewhat after those of the University of Virginia. They formed a square composed of a classroom building two stories high, fronted with a portico of six Ionic columns and an imposing flight of steps; two faculty buildings, each to house four families and arranged to provide each family with "six large airy rooms," kitchen, and outbuildings; and two dormitories, known as Washington and Jefferson halls. In the center of the square stood the Rotunda, three stories high and surmounted by a dome. Students dined in a handsome two-story brick building behind Washington Hall.

The early years of the University were ones of academic tension, and discipline of the students proved to be a major problem. President Woods, a Harvard graduate, expected the young sons of pioneers "to live up to approximately the same standards of gentlemanly conduct that had obtained at Harvard in the 1820's," and he ruled his students with an iron hand. Relations between faculty and students alternated "between periods of armed truce and periods of open warfare."[1]

Mrs. Woods, whom Sarah Gayle had called "one of the sweetest women I ever saw," endeared herself to the students and served as a buffer between them and her husband on numerous occasions. The presence of young Amelia undoubtedly created some relief from the daily pressures that confronted President and Mrs. Woods. During the time that Amelia remained with them, Mrs. Woods was both mother and teacher for her and treated her "with all the care and tenderness that could have been bestowed on her own child."[2]

The fall of 1837 brought two events that were to affect Amelia's life significantly. Dr. Woods resigned as president of the University to return to intellectual pursuits in his native Rhode Island, and her father remarried and established a home where his children could be reunited. His second wife was twenty-three-year-old Clarissa (Clara) Stedman Peck of Greensboro, the sister-in-law of Sarah Gayle's friend and correspondent Mary Peck.

Settling down in Toulminville, a "pretty village" north of Mobile, the Gayles lived in a comfortable frame house with long galleries across the front and sides. An avenue of cedars led to the home, and handsome live oaks and magnolias shaded the yard. Hetty was still the family's principal servant and relieved Clara Gayle, who soon became "Ma" to all the children, of much of the burden of their care. John Gayle practiced law in Mobile and took an active interest in politics. Already proved to be a "states' rights" advocate in the dispute over the Indian lands, he now aligned himself with the Whig Party, many of whose members were followers of John C. Calhoun and his "strict construction" policy. Calhoun considered himself a "no-party" man, but along with Daniel Webster and Henry Clay, the leading Whigs, he opposed Jackson's policies.[3]

Gayle was determined that all of his children, daughters as well as sons, should receive the best possible education, and desiring opportunities for fifteen-year-old Sarah that were not available in Mobile, he took her north to school in June 1839. The journey began with a boat trip to Pensacola and a visit with Lucinda Eastin and her family, who were now living in the coastal town. Here Sarah "walked out" with the young officers stationed at the naval base there. From Pensacola they went by steamer to La Grange, Georgia, where they took a stage for Greensboro, North Carolina, stopping overnight at Columbia, South Carolina, on the way. Sarah wrote that she found stage travel "infinitely more agreeable" than the train ride from Greensboro to Fredericksburg, Virginia.[4] The grueling trip concluded with a steamboat voyage from Fredericksburg to Washington and a day-long rail journey from there to New York. Sarah and her father stayed at the "Great" Astor House until she was enrolled at

Madame Adele Canda's boarding school, where she was to study for a year.[5]

Sarah saw many Mobile acquaintances during the summer and fall, for a yellow-fever epidemic swept the Southern city, and everyone who could leave the town did so, many traveling as far away as New York. Amelia escaped danger by visiting the Eastins in Pensacola, but her father contracted the disease after his return from New York and caused his family great anxiety for several weeks before he improved. Mrs. Gayle wrote Sarah that twenty to thirty persons were dying every day.

By 1841 Sarah had returned to Mobile, and it was Amelia's turn to be sent away to school. Her father selected the Columbia Female Institute in Columbia, Tennessee, which was very popular with Alabamians, who made up more than half the boarding students. The school had been established in 1836 by Bishop James Hervey Otey, first bishop of the Episcopal Diocese of Tennessee.[6] Mr. Smith, the head of the school, frequently called on Amelia to entertain new students when their parents brought them to be enrolled. Amelia wrote to her sister Sarah, "When he introduces me, he says, 'I will leave you to Miss Gayle she is *so* polite.' I am glad if he thinks so." Amelia studied geography, French, arithmetic, music, and reading. The last, she assured Sarah, was no easy subject: "Mr. Smith pays a great deal of attention to it." She added:

> Mrs. Moore, a teacher of great repute arrived from Philadelphia a few days since. I like her so much, one of the girls commenced talking very improperly of step mothers, she made them stop immediately, said that name ought to be abolished, they were in a delicate situation, and the children ought to do everything in their power to make their home pleasant. I wish she could see our happy family and how very much we love our dear Ma.[7]

Amelia shared her own mother's love of reading aloud, and while at school she made a practice of reading the younger girls a favorite tale each evening. One of the smaller ones always sat on her lap. She sent word to her little sister Maria that she would continue the custom when she came home, promising Maria the seat of honor.

At sixteen Amelia returned to Mobile, ready to take her place in society. She rejoiced with the rest of her family at the engagement of her sister Sarah to Dr. William Bones Crawford, a young physician from Winnsboro, South Carolina, who had an established practice in Mobile. Matt Gayle, who was now a student at the Jefferson Medical School in Philadelphia, probably expressed the feelings of all the Gayles when he wrote Dr. Crawford: "I need not assure you of the pleasure the engagement affords me as Sarah has doubtless informed you of all that I have written her on the subject. I will but add that in my opinion she could not have chosen more wisely. . . ."[8] On the evening of December 6, 1842, the wedding took place in the Gayle home, attended by close friends and relatives who had been sent handwritten invitations to the ceremony. The young couple set up housekeeping in Mobile, and soon there was much visiting back and forth between their home and the Gayle residence in Toulminville.

During the summer of 1843 Amelia went with her family to Pascagoula, Mississippi, about thirty miles southwest of Mobile on the Gulf of Mexico. She wrote Sarah: "Our house, you know, is three stories. Maria with her dolls occupy the *attic*, we have the second story, and a dining room and parlour downstairs, beside pantry, storeroom, etc. Now don't you call that living in style!" Her letter to her sister continued:

> The bathing is delightful and we all enjoy it very much, negroes included excepting old Aunt Levisy and she is so dreadfully afraid the crabs will bite her feet that we cannot prevail upon her to go in. . . . I went up to the hotel yesterday evening to play nine-pins, and succeeded amazingly well. Mr. & Mrs. Field are very kind; they let us have ice and fish whenever we wish. Mrs. King has been threatened for the last day or two with the grippe. If flesh aked instead of bones, would not she suffer? Mrs. Field told us the hotel had been a perfect hospital; servants and boarders all sick at the same time. Ma wrote Pa yesterday and commissioned him to get some things for her but forgot some which she wishes you to tell him of. She wants 1 doz. earthen jars holding half pint, and with lids (Pa can get them at Mr. Caldwell's for 12 ½ ct. apiece)—a bottle of castor oil and some rhubarb. You see we are preparing for la grippe. . . . We are expecting you and Dr. Crawford down every day and have a room all ready for you. Tell Dr.

C. we want him to teach us to swim as Ma will require all of Pa's time
to give her lessons in the art. . . . The wind is blowing very hard and I
see some streaks of lightning so I will just jump in bed. Goodnight.[9]

The following winter Sarah Crawford's first child, Clara Jane,
was born, and Governor Gayle and his wife became the parents of a
son, Frederick. As the oldest daughter at home, Amelia found a
great deal to keep her busy. Children loved her, and "her very
presence seemed to soothe the sick."[10] In addition there was much to
interest her in the life of Mobile, which was now a thriving seaport
of 15,000. Since 1823 it had had a theater where performances by
touring companies could be seen. According to a correspondent of
the New Orleans *Observer*, the cultural center of the city at this
period was the Franklin Society, which offered a reading room with
a "good" library and the beginnings of an archaeological collection.
Meetings were held in the hall for the discussion of literary and
scientific subjects, and from time to time distinguished speakers
from other parts of the country delivered lectures there.[11]

Throughout the 1840s Amelia must have followed with interest
the political activities of her father. He was the unsuccessful Whig
candidate for the Senate in 1840 and a Whig elector in the presiden-
tial contest between William Henry Harrison and Martin Van Bu-
ren. When Henry Clay visited Mobile in 1843, Gayle made the
address of welcome at a reception given at the Mansion House in
Clay's honor. Most significant for Amelia, however, was her father's
election in 1847 to the United States House of Representatives, for it
was decided that Clara Gayle would remain in Alabama to care for
her two young children and that Amelia would accompany her
father to Washington.[12]

3

WASHINGTON CITY

THE TRIP NORTH from Mobile had not changed a great deal in the eight years since Governor Gayle accompanied his daughter Sarah to New York. One of the common routes took the traveler by way of Montgomery to Augusta, Georgia, and north through Richmond, Virginia. This route must have been Amelia's path, for the Richmond *Whig* of November 30, 1847, noted the arrival at Powhatan House of "Governor Gayle and Daughter, Alabama."[1]

When the Gayles arrived in Washington, they took rooms in one of the numerous boarding houses frequented by members of Congress. Living at the same "mess" were Senator John C. Calhoun, his niece, Martha Calhoun Burt, and her husband, Armistead Burt, who represented South Carolina in the House of Representatives. A courtly gentleman of sixty-five when Amelia met him, Calhoun was renowned as a favorite of the fair sex. A contemporary said of him, "In the company of ladies this austere figure was one of the most interesting and charming in the world."[2] Mrs. Jefferson Davis was captivated by the senator on her first meeting with him in 1845, and he won the complete admiration of the young English traveler, Sarah Mytton Maury, who wrote in her *Statesmen of America in 1846:* "Calhoun is my Statesman. Through good report and through evil report; in all his doctrines, whether upon Slavery, Free Trade, Nullification, Treasury and Currency Systems, Active Annexation or *Masterly inactivity*, I hold myself his avowed and admiring disciple."[3]

Calhoun apparently took a great fancy to Amelia, who was at twenty-one a slender, graceful brunette with a keen wit, and he treated her almost as if she had been his own daughter. She wrote Sarah Crawford, "My room opens immediately into Mr. Calhoun's

& he says when the weather grows warm we will throw the doors open & give me the benefit of his South windows."[4]

An amusing incident occurred during Henry Clay's stay in Washington in January 1848. Clay, like Calhoun, was much admired by the female residents of the capital city; "matrons saved as relics the gloves he pressed and young ladies kissed him in public."[5] One evening he called to see Senator Calhoun. Amelia greeted him at the door, and Clay, mistaking her for Martha Burt, gave her a kiss of greeting. Amelia, flushed with excitement, exclaimed, "Oh, Mr. Calhoun, I have been kissed by the great Senator Clay." Calhoun replied with great solemnity, "Amelia, don't put your trust in that old man."[6]

Quickly becoming involved in many aspects of Washington life, Amelia acquired keen interest in politics and in the speech-making efforts of her particular friends. Sarah Mytton Maury noted this interest in many of the wives and friends of members of Congress when she wrote:

> I shared in their anxious hopes and fears that our many favorites should go through the ordeal with honor. We always went together to the Supreme Court, the Senate, or the House to listen to their speeches and to cheer them by our presence.... The intercourse between the statesmen and politicians of all parties and the ladies was of the most agreeable kind, and to the latter it was a source of great instruction and improvement, for nothing elevates and corrects the female mind more than the friendship of distinguished men.[7]

Amelia's primary concern was, of course, with her father's career, and she wrote enthusiastically to Sarah Crawford of his first address to Congress on March 28, 1848. He spoke on an amendment to the bill to establish the territorial government of Oregon, a crucial issue to Southerners because it involved the right of slave owners to take slaves into new territories:

> Pa made his maiden speech in the house yesterday and our gentlemen say did extremely well. I am sorry that I did not hear him for I felt the greatest anxiety that he should succeed in his first attempt to make himself heard in Congress. I think Pa is rather gratified with the impression he made and particularly pleased with the congratulations

of some of his political opponents. The speech will be published in a pamphlet form in a few days when I will direct you a copy.[8]

Before beginning his speech Gayle had addressed the House, saying that the written speech he held in his hand would take about forty minutes to deliver. If the members were content to give him their quiet attention for that length of time, he said, he would confine himself to the manuscript, but if not, he would lay aside his written speech and address them without it, in which case he would claim the full hour allowed him. This offer of a bargain was greeted with laughter and cries of "agreed, agreed."[9]

Although Amelia did not hear her father's first speech, she did visit the Congress on other occasions, and her report of one debate shows her intense involvement with the issues of the day:

> The slavery question has been introduced into the house & as you may imagine produces great excitement. I listened to the most animated debates there on Friday & could scarcely keep my seat when the abolitionists would rise & avow themselves openly the partizans of the negroes.[10]

She also followed with interest the activities of the other members of the Alabama delegation. Among them was Senator Dixon Hall Lewis, who weighed four hundred and thirty pounds and was reported to have paid for—and filled—two seats on the mail coaches whenever he traveled to Washington. Lewis was provided with a special chair on the floor of the Senate, just as he had been years earlier when he served in the Alabama Legislature in Tuscaloosa.[11] Another friend was Representative Henry W. Hilliard of Alabama, an eloquent Whig who had served as chargé d'affaires in Belgium under President John Tyler. Amelia wrote her sister:

> Mr. Hilliard from our state has joined our mess within the last few days & is I assure you a most delightful acquisition to our small family. His residence abroad gives him access to the houses of all the foreign ministers in Washington & as he has placed himself entirely at our disposal we will be enabled to attend more frequently the evening soirées of these dignitaries.

Amelia's reaction to the uprising in France in February 1848 indicates the interest she developed in "these dignitaries":

> The revolution in France as you may well imagine produced the
> greatest excitement among the dependents of that Gov. in
> Washington. M. Pageot the French minister has been dismissed by
> the present French ministry, & will be compelled to retire to some
> estates of his wife's in Tennessee. The Attachès are all in the greatest
> consternation, being entirely dependent on their offices for support in
> this country & they do not dare until difficulties are settled to return
> to France. By many it is surmised that Louis Philippe will take refuge
> once more in this country. He has valuable property in the City [of]
> New York & from the revenue which it affords him will be enabled to
> live there in fitting style for a banished king.

Domestic politics and foreign affairs were not the only diversions
"Washington City" offered to Amelia. On March 30 she and Martha
Burt spent the day with the "Crittendon Mess," who, she wrote
Sarah, "have taken a handsome house in the Court end of the city."
Amelia described Kentucky's John J. Crittenden, a leading Whig:

> Mr. Crittendon sat by me at dinner & would have been vastly agree-
> able if he had not kept me in an agony for fear my new dress would be
> ruined with his *tobacco juice*, which he constantly expectorated even at
> the table. He is a lively good natured old man & loves dearly to play
> his jokes off on the girls.

Amelia also wrote her sister that Mrs. Robert Toombs, wife of the
senator from Georgia, kept a carriage and horses and had very kindly
offered the use of them whenever she and Mrs. Burt felt "inclined to
take an airing." They were not exclusively dependent on driving for
amusement and fresh air, however, as Amelia noted:

> The favorite & fashionable walk at this season is through the Capitol
> grounds which really offer every inducement that art and good taste
> can invent to tempt us idle members to sun ourselves of a bright
> afternoon. And what to my eye completes the charm of the fairy scene
> is the number of beautiful children who are carried there from all
> parts of the city to romp & roll over the smooth green-sward which is
> kept as clean as any parlour floor. If Clara & Milly could only be

transplanted here with how much pride & pleasure I would watch their gambols.

Above all Amelia enjoyed her frequent strolls with Calhoun. On the first of April:

> Mr. Calhoun tapped at my door this morning for me to take a long walk with him before breakfast. Fortunately I was awake & soon dressed for I enjoy of all things a walk with him. We discussed the French revolution—its probable effects upon all Europe, the destina- tion & final settlement of the royal family etc., etc.—then by a strange transition, we talked of housekeeping & he gratified me by saying that of all things in the world he disliked an over-particular house-wife, nothing to him was half so annoying. We walked about an hour & returned with keen appetites for breakfast & a fine color in my cheeks.

The only deficiency Amelia found in Washington's social life was the inferiority of its theatrical offerings compared to those of Mobile. She wrote that Washington offered no inducement to good actresses in any branch of the profession to make engagements. "There is only one small theatre about the size of your two parlours—attended generally by the lowest class of women which of course prevents our amusing ourselves there by their absurd acting."[12]

Late in April the Gayles, the Burts, and Senator Calhoun decided to set up housekeeping together in a house on F Street between 13th and 14th streets, just a few blocks from the White House. Amelia commented in a letter to her brother Matt, "It is far more comforta- ble & equally as cheap as boarding—we pay $75. a month for the house completely furnished & in a delightful & healthy location, sufficiently far from the Capitol to give the gentlemen plenty of exercise."[13]

The Gayles remained in Washington throughout most of the summer of 1848; Congress did not adjourn until August 14. During this election year John Gayle followed closely the campaign for the Whig nomination for president. Although Henry Clay was his first choice, Gayle gave his enthusiastic support to the party's nominees, Zachary Taylor and Millard Fillmore.

While the campaign was getting under way over the country,

Congress continued to struggle with problems of state, and on June 27, 1848, Calhoun made one of his most impassioned speeches. Armistead Burt sent the following account of it to the Charleston *Mercury:*

> It is Tuesday and one of the hottest days ever known in this sweltering climate. I have just left the Senate chamber. It is crowded—packed to the point of suffocation. The fair and the brave, the grave and the gay are here. A feather might be heard to fall on the meeting of the Chamber. Every head is turned and every eye directed towards the tall figure of one who now holds this mighty audience spell-bound and speechless and motionless. It is the great Carolinian—it is John C. Calhoun, who alone on such a day could assemble such an audience. It was a spectacle to look upon, and to make the heart of Carolina swell with honest pride. The Oregon bill was the occasion—the exclusion of slavery the subject. Such a noble vindication of the South—such an inspiring exhibition of Roman patriotism, has never been witnessed since the days of the Revolution. Would to Heaven every Southern man—every Northern man—every patriot—could have heard this masterly display of a noble love of country in this mighty effort of the greatest intellect of that country.
>
> Addressing himself to the Southern Senators after a magnificent burst of indignant eloquence against the ostracism of the South, in a tone of deep solemnity he asked, "Will you submit to this degredation? If you will, you have wofully degenerated from your sires."
>
> So say we, so will every man who dares not dishonor his manhood.[14]

Amelia probably shared Burt's feelings on this occasion. She placed his account of it in her scrapbook along with other mementoes of her Washington stay: an autographed woodcut of Dixon Lewis, an invitation to Burt from the Russian ambassador, Baron Alexander Bodisco, and a flattering note to Calhoun from a man who had served under him in the War Department.

On the Fourth of July there was a break in the legislative routine, and much of Washington's populace turned out for the laying of the cornerstone of the Washington Monument. Amelia was invited by Calhoun to sit on the platform to witness the activities, which included a parade to the site, a speech by the Honorable Robert C. Winthrop, Speaker of the House of Representatives, and an elaborate Masonic ritual conducted by Benjamin French, grand master of the Masonic fraternity of the District of Columbia. French used the trowel with which George Washington had laid the cornerstone of the capitol nearly fifty years earlier. The exercises were conducted in the presence of President James K. Polk, members of Congress and the Judiciary, representatives of foreign governments, and many others. Dolley Madison and Mrs. Alexander Hamilton were special guests. The day was bright and sunny and the parade impressive, with many military units and fire departments, the Independent Order of Odd Fellows, the Order of Redmen, and representatives of temperance societies—even a wagon bearing a large cask of cold water, inscribed "Fountain of Health."[15]

It must have been with real regret that Amelia left Washington at the end of the summer even to rejoin her beloved family in Alabama, for she clearly relished the opportunities the city offered her, and she had made a place for herself in capital society through her own wit and charm.

YELLOW FEVER
AIDS CUPID

Amelia traveled south as far as Richmond in the company of Secretary of the Navy John Y. Mason and his wife, who had been called home to Virginia by the illness of one of their children. Amelia tried to be of some help to Mrs. Mason on the journey, and she also spoke to the secretary of her hope that her brother Richard might secure admission to the Naval Academy. A short time after her return to Mobile, she received the following letter from Secretary Mason, dated September 2, 1848.

> I send you permission for your brother to come to Annapolis to be examined preparatory to his admission as a midshipman of the Navy. I am happy to gratify your wishes and doubt not that I am securing to the Navy a gallant and meritorious officer.
>
> After leaving you, we found our dear child living and conscious. He knew us and tho' he never smiled, he evinced by his looks his recognition and tender affection. He lingered until Sunday, the 20th and breathed his last without a struggle. He sleeps by the side of his little brother who had gone before him, in our garden at home. I know your kind heart will sympathize with his afflicted Mother.
>
> I am deeply indebted to you for your affectionate attention to her on our journey.[1]

Amelia must have been distressed for her friends in the loss of their child, but news of this opportunity for Dick was welcome indeed. Such encounters as this one with Mr. Mason demonstrate graphically the force of Amelia's personality.

Interest in politics was keen during the fall. John Gayle and his fellow Alabama Whigs were almost successful in their efforts to carry the state for Taylor, but the Democrat Cass won by fewer than one thousand votes in the closest contest between the two parties in Alabama history.[2]

John Gayle returned to Washington in December 1848, this time leaving Amelia behind. He wrote his wife that he had to make excuses for his daughter's absence to her many friends and that he had told them she stayed at home because Mobile was to be very festive that winter. He did not like to give the real reason—that he could not afford to bring her again. His generous nature and the demands of so large a family combined to bring about his straitened circumstances. Shortly after his inauguration President Zachary Taylor appointed John Gayle to the United States District Court for Alabama as judge at a salary of $2500 a year. This appointment brought a certain amount of security to the Gayles and met with general approval from the public. From this time he took no further part in politics, following the custom that judges remove themselves from the political arena.

The Gayle household now included four grown or nearly grown young women, Amelia, her sisters Mary and Maria, and their first cousin Anne Gayle.[3] Their social life was lively. When there were balls to attend in the city, the girls often stayed with the Crawfords. At other times the gentlemen drove out in their buggies to call at Toulminville.

The Crawford children were also frequent visitors, feeling almost as much as home at their grandfather's as at their parents' house in town. Amelia was "Aunt Amelia" to them and to their cousins, the children of their father's brother, James Crawford. A great favorite with her friends' children as well, she was often called on to sit with a sick baby or to assist at a birthday party. Years later James Crawford's daughter Mary recalled attending an elaborate birthday celebration given for young Isaac Bell III, whose mother Adelaide was one of Amelia's closest friends. After supper, magic lantern pictures were planned for the guests' amusement, but the party almost ended in disaster, for the children had never seen slides before, and the room was filled with frightened screams when the lights were extinguished for the show to begin. Calm was restored with reassurances from Amelia and Ikey's mother.[4]

In the spring of 1849 Amelia assumed full responsibility for the three Crawford children to enable Sarah to accompany her sick husband on a trip his doctors had prescribed for him.[5] Sarah mentioned in the journal she kept during her travels that Amelia was really a second mother to her children, taking "all the care in the world of them."

Frequently during her journey Sarah wrote home, describing the people she met and the places she visited and sharing with her family her anxiety over her husband's health. In Richmond the Crawfords stayed at the Powhatan House, where Amelia and Governor Gayle had stopped en route to Washington eighteen months before. While in Richmond they called on Governor John B. Floyd, who had been a classmate of Dr. Crawford's at South Carolina College. Sarah described the governor's residence near the capitol as a "fine brick home in the midst of highly improved grounds."

Amelia must have been especially interested in Sarah's reaction to Washington. From the Willard Hotel in the city Sarah wrote: "At the table we sit with three or four distinguished persons—Vice-president Fillmore at the head and Truman Smith at his side—Mr. Evans from Maine opposite us. Mr. Fillmore has a pleasant face—not particularly indicative of strong talent, but kind and agreeable. Mr. Webster is expected in town today."[6]

On June 9 the Crawfords attended the president's levee, which Sarah described in great detail.

> I had been deterred from visiting Gen. Taylor by a feeling of timidity and actually shrunk back that night but as soon as I saw how full the room was & how unnoticed the ordinary personages were, I felt no further hesitation. Gen. Taylor stood near the center of the room when we entered, and as soon as there was something of a pause, the Dr. presented me as Gov. Gayle's daughter. The old general was very courteous, and after exchanging a few commonplace remarks, & inquiring after Pa—we bowed and made room for others who were behind us. The President approached and addressed himself to me two or three different times afterward, so that I saw he remembered me. For an old soldier, & one too so little noted for parlor manners, I think he does the honors of the house with great ease. His figure is more thin than before his installation & those

previously acquainted, say he looks care worn. He seems easy—pays pretty compliments to all the ladies.

Sarah was also introduced to the president's daughter:

> Mrs. Bliss—well known as Miss Betty Taylor stood near the entrance and received the company with remarkable elegance and composure—She is a very pretty woman I think, about my size—fine eyes—tho' her face by no means striking. She was very simply dressed in a white dotted swiss muslin dress, made very much in the New Orleans style—high necked—short sleeves—black lace gloves & several bracelets.

Sarah noted that Dolley Madison, with whom Amelia had shared the platform the year before, "was a centre of attraction almost as great as the President himself":

> There stood the old lady of seven scores [*sic*] of years—at least—a tall elegant woman—still full and commanding in her person and dressed peculiarly. Her face is fine, features large & rather masculine perhaps—she must have been rouged—wore her own gray hair parted on her brow & surmounted with a white satin turban, ornamented by a very large magnificent diamond brooch in the front. Her dress was of figured black silk—made very low in the neck—somewhat of the old style with square shoulder straps—I think—Her fine fair fat neck and bosom were covered with a gossamer like inside cape—finished off with a quilling of thulle close up around the throat & she wore also an elegant white lace or blond scarf carelessly around her shoulders—She extended her small aristocratic white gloved hand to me. I felt an emotion of reverence for her & was proud of the honor of pressing her hand. I did not know what to say & escaped among the crowd.

Amelia kept the Crawfords informed of their children's well-being, writing them in New York that Clara, whose health had always been frail, seemed to be improving in the country. From Boston Sarah wrote of receiving "a blessed budget of letters from home" recording in her journal: "My heart fairly leaped with joy at the good news from my dear children & all my family. Indeed I feel how nearly knit together we all are at home. My sisters I love tenderly, and there is nothing I have that I do not wish them to enjoy & if I could without injustice to the Dr's purse I would like to carry home many pretty things for them which I cannot. They do not measure my love by gifts tho' for they know we are not rich enough."

Before starting south again the Crawfords stopped in Newport, Rhode Island, to visit Mrs. Alva Woods, whom Sarah had not seen since the Woods had left Tuscaloosa almost twelve years earlier. "How we did revel in the reminiscences of years past—how we wept and laughed over things past by—She expressed particular anxiety to hear of Sister Amelia who after all was her favorite and deservedly so—for she adored Mrs. W." Sarah gave Mrs. Woods a bracelet woven of Amelia's and her own hair, which "gratified her very much." She described her hostess in her journal as "a Bostonian by birth & education—and a most warm-hearted & whole souled Yankee."[7]

To indulge her desire to do something for her sisters, Sarah bought silk dresses to give Mary and Amelia on her return to Mobile in September. Much to the relief of the whole family Dr. Crawford then seemed well enough to take up his practice again. The winter of 1849–50 passed pleasantly. The Gayle girls were much admired, though their cousin Mrs. Jabez Heustis said they held their heads so high that they could find no one they deemed their equal and seemed to fear they would remain spinsters.[8]

In March Amelia was able to gratify her taste for the theater when Mobile was the scene of two weeks of ballet, followed by two weeks of drama. Charlotte Cushman, well known for her Shakespearian characterizations, received star billing. Amelia saved Miss Cushman's autograph, secured on the night of her final Mobile performance as Rosalind in *As You Like It*. Although Miss Cushman had won her first great acclaim in New Orleans in 1836 and was received enthusiastically throughout the South on her 1850 tour, she had little good to say of that part of the country, finding its towns "ragged," its contrasts disturbing, and travel uncomfortable.[9]

On April 1, 1850, the *Mobile Daily Register* carried the following article:

It becomes our painful duty to announce the death of the distinguished statesman and patriot, John C. Calhoun. He died at
Washington yesterday morning at 7 o'clock. The telegraphic dispatch
conveying this melancholy intelligence reached us at half past four
o'clock yesterday evening.

The loss of a citizen so distinguished, and who filled so large a space
in the public eye, would at any time awaken the profoundest sensa-
tions, but that he should be called from his post at such a critical
period in public affairs, gives particular point to the dispensation, and
will cause it to be regarded as a national infliction.[10]

Amelia must have been deeply distressed at the death of her old
friend, whose last words were reported to have been, "The South,
the poor South, God knows what will become of her."[11]

During the following summer Amelia visited Bladon Springs, a
popular watering place advertised extravagantly in the *Mobile Daily
Register:* "The medical properties of the water are too long and well
established to need anything more than a reference to them. . . . All
persons suffering from disease and debility brought on by long residence and close confinement in our cities in this warm climate benefit from these waters." Sometimes called the "Saratoga of the
South," Bladon Springs had a hotel, completed in 1846, that housed
two hundred guests.[12]

As was to be expected in a large family in which there was such a
wide disparity in ages, the next few years were marked by marriages
and births in the Gayle family. The marriage of Anne Gayle to
Richard Owen, a promising young Mobile lawyer, and the birth of
John and Clara Gayle's second son, John Marshall, were highlights
of 1850. In December 1852 the Gayles rejoiced in Mary's marriage
to Hugh Kerr Aiken of Winnsboro, South Carolina, who was a
friend of the Crawford family. When Hugh had visited Mobile on
business, he had been introduced to his future bride by Captain
James Crawford. At their wedding in the dining room of the Gayle
home, Amelia was bridesmaid and mistress of ceremonies.

The following spring Amelia went North for a visit, in New York
with Dr. and Mrs. Valentine Mott, parents of her friend Adelaide
Bell, and in Providence with Dr. and Mrs. Woods. She returned
home at the end of June to find the whole family alarmed over Dr.

Crawford's rapidly declining health. His physician, Dr. Josiah Nott, his brother James Crawford, and Judge Gayle all advised further travel. Sarah's family again offered to keep her children so that she could accompany her husband. Her son Billy went to his Uncle James' plantation in Greene County, while Clara, Amelia's namesake Milly, and baby Sallie, who had been born in January, were left at the Gayles "under the careful supervision of Sister Amelia."

The Crawfords met Mary and Hugh Aiken briefly in Charleston, then went on to New York, where they engaged passage for Liverpool. Sarah found New York rather trying: "The noise of the streets of N. Y. exceeds anything I ever knew. We can scarcely take any rest at night in consequence. People never seem to repose here. All night long the streets are resounding with the rattling of carriages over the stony streets." She and her husband spent a few days in England, then reluctantly went on to France. Sarah wrote, "I regret the climate is so bad that the Dr. suffers from the effects of it so I leave before I have begun to see the many objects of exceeding interest in London."[13]

By midsummer yellow fever, that scourge of Southern cities, had again reached epidemic proportions in Mobile. The cause of the disease was still unknown, though some physicians, Dr. Josiah Nott among them, were suggesting an insect origin.[14] People believed that higher elevations were fairly safe places of refuge, and in late August Judge Gayle arranged for Amelia and Maria to take the Crawford children to Mount Vernon Arsenal about thirty miles north of Mobile, where Matthew Gayle was post surgeon. The arsenal was situated on high dry ground three miles above the west bank of the Mobile River.

Matt's quarters adjoined those of the arsenal's commanding officer, Josiah Gorgas, a thirty-five-year-old lieutenant from Pennsylvania. It was natural that Lieutenant Gorgas should make the acquaintance of the visitors. He was immediately charmed by Amelia, whose lovely voice attracted him as he heard her reading aloud to the children on the neighboring porch even before he was introduced to her.[15] Their friendship soon developed into a much deeper relationship.

Born at Running Pumps, Pennsylvania, on July 1, 1818, Josiah

Gorgas was the youngest of the ten children of Joseph and Sophia Atkinson Gorgas. His parents had struggled to support their large family, moving to several different Pennsylvania towns in search of a successful living. At seventeen Josiah went to live with his sister Eliza and her husband, Daniel Chapman, in Lyons, New York, and became an apprentice at the printing office of the Lyons's *Carrier's Address*. There he was befriended by Graham Chapin, a lawyer and congressman who took him into his office to read law and then recommended him for appointment to West Point, believing the young man deserved a college education.

Josiah entered the Military Academy in 1837 and was graduated sixth in his class of fifty-two in June 1841. Electing to serve in the ordnance corps, he was sent to Watervliet Arsenal at Troy, New York. In 1845 he obtained leave to travel in Europe, where he increased his knowledge of foreign ordnance and indulged his interest in art by visiting as many museums as he could.

He served under General Winfield Scott in Mexico in 1847 and was head of the ordnance depot at Vera Cruz, where he suffered a mild case of yellow fever during the epidemic that swept the city during the summer. In January 1848 he wrote his mother that as soon as he got back to the United States he would get married, provided he could find someone whom she would approve and who would have him. After his return and several brief tours, he was sent in 1851 to Fort Monroe Arsenal in Virginia.[16]

From Fort Monroe Gorgas was sent to Mount Vernon in Alabama. Within a few weeks he was writing to his superior officer that he would "not be reconciled to a long residence at the South, and I beg you therefore to take this opportunity to give me a post at the North." He continued, "The absence of all society neutralizes to a bachelor the advantages which make it a pleasant residence to a family."[17] Amelia's arrival in August remedied that "absence of all society," and no more was heard about the young officer's desire to leave the South.

In October Amelia received the following acrostic:

To Amelia—
    Ah! lovely friend—the verse you claim
    Mingled each number with your name—

Ever dear!—that name will be
Life, love, hopes, fears—all—to me
I feel its power—I own its spell
And I must love—too well—too well.[18]

Early in August, Maria Gayle had written to Sarah that her "affair
de cour" [*sic*] was likely to progress and terminate happily, and now
it seemed that Amelia, too, had found the person to whom she could
give her heart.

Amelia's personal happiness must have been tempered by grave
concern about her brother-in-law, for reports from Sarah were not
encouraging. From Paris she wrote, "The Dr. does not seem to
improve tho' as we expected. I fear for him!" They began to talk of
returning nearer home for the winter, perhaps to the West Indies.
Meanwhile Dr. Crawford was determined that his wife should see
some of the sights of Paris that he had enjoyed while he was there
studying medicine, and he sent her with Alabama friends to Ver-
sailles, St. Cloud, and the Opera, where she saw Queen Christina of
Spain and her two daughters in the imperial box. Sarah was not
altogether pleased with Paris, which she called "this pleasure seeking
and God forgetting metropolis."

Sarah's journal for October 8 notes her having received a letter
from Amelia that gave a "lively, glowing picture" of the children, but
not, apparently, any mention of her new admirer. Amelia's responsibility for her nieces was to last for several more months. The
Crawfords were unable to secure passage to the West Indies and
instead began a leisurely journey southward to Malaga, Spain, paus-
ing at Fontainebleau and at Lyons, where Sarah observed: "Women
& children I see everywhere in France working out in the fields. The
females do a great deal of the hardest work—I always felt a great
regret & pity at seeing negro women working in the field—but they
were not so roughly clad, nor more exposed to weather than the
working class here."[19]

The yellow fever epidemic in Mobile was a constant source of
anxiety to Sarah and her husband, all the more since news from
home often took a month to reach them. Dr. Crawford wrote his
father-in-law, "I was very much pleased to hear that Amelia had
taken the children to Mt. Vernon and hope that you with the rest of

the family are spending the time of the epidemic in that elevated healthy location."[20] Their concern was magnified by the tragic news of the death of four of the children of their physician and friend, Dr. Josiah Nott. Sarah wrote:

> This is an awful blow, and I do not see what on earth supports them under such an afflictive visitation. Nothing save the belief in a wise Providence & a firm belief in his love & justice can bring resignation to stricken hearts like theirs must be—Poor poor crushed parents—how sincerely we do lament with them in their loss. Dr. Nott—always so sympathetic—so regardful of the feelings of others—to be thus sorely tried. . . . He has been ever our unchanging friend!

This sad news from home was almost more than Sarah could bear. Her husband was losing ground daily, and he told her that he regarded his case as hopeless. "Oh Heaven! What shall I do?" she wrote: "It is terrible this idea of having to anticipate an event & so agonizing to look on so calmly as he does at what he considers inevitable."

In November the Crawfords settled down in a hotel in Malaga. The American consul and his family called on them soon after their arrival and offered them any assistance they might need. "It is a good thing to be able to claim one friend in a strange place," wrote Sarah.[21] They talked of crossing to Cuba from Spain, but Dr. Crawford was having to depend on opiates almost nightly to get any rest, and even as they discussed returning to Mobile, dread hung over them.

WIFE AND MOTHER

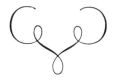

IT WAS ESTIMATED that during the ninety-day yellow-fever epidemic in the summer and fall of 1853 fifteen hundred persons died in Mobile.[1] With the coming of cool weather, however, the threat of the dread disease passed for another year, and Amelia and her charges returned to the city.

Plans were soon under way for two family weddings. On December 22 Maria would marry Thomas Levingston Bayne, a native of Georgia, an honor graduate of Yale, and at twenty-nine a successful lawyer in New Orleans. Amelia's marriage to Josiah was to be solemnized a week later on December 29. Mary and Hugh Aiken came from South Carolina to be present for the ceremonies. Only the discouraging news of Dr. Crawford's failing health cast a shadow on this otherwise happy time.

Both weddings took place at Christ Episcopal Church in downtown Mobile. The rector of the parish, the Reverend Nathaniel Knapp, performed the morning ceremony at which Amelia Ross Gayle became the wife of Josiah Gorgas. The bride wore a light-lilac silk dress and matching bonnet trimmed with pink roses.[2] Immediately after the wedding, the couple left for Mount Vernon Arsenal, where a reception was planned in their honor.[3]

Having done everything he could to make his quarters at the Arsenal as attractive as possible for Amelia, Josiah even secured permission to plant a vegetable garden on the grounds. Amelia rejoiced at being able to make for her husband the home that he had missed during the early years of his army life. Josiah wrote his friend John Hillhouse, the traveling companion of his European trip, about his marriage, giving him a "verbal daguerreotype" of his new wife:

To begin at the beginning: she is just five feet two and one-half inches high; exactly the height of the Venus de Medicis, a copy of which, you may recollect, I so carefully measured in the Bodleian Library at Oxford. Next, these five feet two and one-half inches include a very taper waist, and a very pretty foot and ankle; and the whole, when in motion, is decidedly graceful in its movements. Her complexion is brunette—which infers dark hair and eyes—and these latter are large and prononcées; from which you may conclude, without danger of contradiction, that she has the organ of language largely developed, and knows how to use her mother tongue. Her mouth is large and good-natured, and does only one thing better than talking. To conclude this brief sketch of her appearance, let me add, that it gives rise to the only subject of difference between us: she insists on calling this better half of myself, plain—an aspersion which I repel with animation. Whether my eyes, or her mirror, presents the truest picture, you will judge for yourself when you see her. . . .

The husband's praises of his new wife's character were as lavish as those of her appearance:

She has . . . that spirit of charity, which, if it does not embrace all the female virtues, leads to many of them. Almost my first acquaintance with her was by the bed-side of a brave little boy, the child of a man of my command, whose young existence was already closing; its life fast ebbing away amid the agonies of a dreaded disease—the yellow fever. An errand of duty on my part, and of benevolence on hers, took us there; and the little sufferer died in her arms. . . . She greets her friends with a smile, and is never ill-tempered with a somewhat impatient husband. . . . Like most women who are graceful, she enjoys dancing, and is devoted to parties, and even balls; yet her face is none the less cheerful, because we live away from all such amusements. She is hospitable—a common virtue with Southern gentlefolk—and is never happier, than when her table is well supplied with guests. . . . She is industrious by nature, and supervises her household affairs personally. She is kind and considerate towards her servants, and studies how she can give them a new pleasure. If it may be called a fault, she has that of being too indulgent to her domestics; she lacks the decision which a house keeper must, I suppose, exercise. But is not that . . . a leaning toward virtue? Might not the decided mistress become the occasionally determined spouse?[4]

Josiah suggested that he and Hillhouse continue their correspondence, reminiscing about their travels and sharing their
memories with their wives by reading the letters aloud during the
winter evenings. He and Amelia also enjoyed reading the current
novels together, and Josiah prepared several translations of French
and German works for her.[5]

Not long after her marriage Amelia received a letter from Sarah,
written in late November, which must have prepared her to expect
news of Dr. Crawford's death. He died in Malaga, Spain, on December 28, but word did not reach the family until February, just a
few days before Sarah completed her solitary journey home to
Mobile. Amelia and Josiah had little Sallie with them at Mount
Vernon, and with Matt Gayle they hurried to Toulminville as soon
as they heard of Sarah's arrival. Sarah was now able to release the
grief which she had had to control for so long among strangers and to
find comfort in the loving support of the father she adored, his wife,
and her brothers and sisters. Always a close family, the Gayles were
drawn even closer by this tragedy.

After a brief stay in Mobile, the Gorgases returned to Mount
Vernon. Josiah had been ordered by Colonel H. K. Craig, the chief
of Ordnance, to inspect Fort Pickens in Pensacola and Fort Morgan
near Mobile. His recommendations for repairs were approved, and
in April 1854 he went to Pensacola to supervise the work. Amelia
reluctantly stayed behind, for she was expecting their first child.
Her friends the Isaac Bells came up from Mobile to be with her
during part of her husband's absence, but they could not entirely
dispel her anxieties. She wrote Sarah:

> Your little note by Mr. Shepherd was brought in by the guard last
> night at 1 o'clock. I was somewhat startled as the man said he was
> ordered to deliver it immediately & I presumed of course contained
> summons to the sick bed of some member of the family—I hope that
> dream is not prophetic. I am not likely to have hysterics but find that
> unusual excitement or fatigue is anything but beneficial to me—I was
> in bed all day yesterday & in so much pain that I thought my antici-
> pated troubles must have a speedy termination—my invaluable little
> book advised me to keep very quiet & to recline upon the bed as much
> as possible giving such plain directions in case of miscarriage that I felt

almost competent to physic myself without the mortification of consulting brother Matt who has not a suspicion of my ailing—This morning however I feel much better, have no other pain than a little back-ache which will pass away with another day's quiet. I fatigued myself unnecessarily in going twice on the tower and over the arsenal.... But be assured if I were ill the grass would not grow under the feet of the horse dispatched for you. I should like of all things to meet Mr. Gorgas in Mobile but dread the drive to Citronelle & still more the two hours on the cars.

I think I can safely promise myself a visit when he goes to Fort Morgan & hope to persuade Mrs. Crawford to return with me. The arsenal looks much better than when you were up & will be charming in another fortnight.

Dick goes down by the early train of cars promising some young ladies to accompany them to Mrs. Mastins Party tomorrow evening.[6] I am sorry he took the trouble to come up since he came only to bring my package—Mt. Vernon I know is too dull for him & I cannot in reason urge him to remain though I am only too happy to have him with us—He has driven Choctaw twice in our little new wagon & all pronounce him an admirable buggy horse—after he is well broken I shall amuse myself driving over these fine hills with Louise for company if you do not lend me one or two of the housefull of urchins at home. The weather is grown quite warm again & I think will increase steadily until the heat of Mobile drives you all to my cool home—I wish I could add a log to the fire by way of expediting your movements. Mrs. Bell quite alarmed me by saying she was convinced I must be in Mobile by the *first of October* if I intended being confined down there—I have a fit of *shivering* whenever I realize the approach of danger & suffering from which there is no withdrawal. I acknowledge my fears for the result but try not to allow them to affect my spirits though poor Julia——& other unfortunate mothers continually present themselves to me—I shall take courage & make all necessary arrangements when I come down—such as engaging a nurse etc.—I am afraid Aunt Hetty will feel hurt that I do not depend upon her, but I think she is too old & infirm to undergo the fatigue of such a troublesome patient as I shall prove—Hannah I think will suit me better & relieve me from all anxiety—I take time by the forelock do I not?...

Maria seems as happy as the day is long & I doubt if she can bear a separation from Mr. Bayne even in June—if she has only a given time to spend at home you must all come up here & give me a benefit at the same time. I would convert the sitting room into a bed chamber for the time being. . . . I wish I could join you at church today—[7]

William Crawford Gorgas was born at Judge Gayle's home in Toulminville on October 3, 1854, with Dr. Josiah Nott in attendance. The child was named for Amelia's beloved brother-in-law, an indication of Josiah's willingness to rely on his wife's judgment on such matters—he had never met Dr. Crawford. At the age of thirty-six Josiah became a doting father, finding it hard to believe his good fortune. In December he wrote to his wife, who had gone back to Mobile for a visit: "Where do you bundle away Willie during your 'sporting' times—Better send him to me—I'm afraid you'll go off to the Theatre & forget you have a boy to nurse." He closed the letter, "Good-by—kiss dear little Willie for papa—Nonsense, I'm not a papa—I can't realize it."[8]

During the winter and spring of 1855 Josiah was occupied with the repair of Fort Barrancas and made frequent trips to Pensacola. His family passed the summer pleasantly at Mount Vernon with many visitors coming from Mobile. Especially delighted in being at the Arsenal, the Crawford children made a plaything of Willie, now at a most appealing age, and reveled in picking blackberries for Josiah's favorite pie.

Josiah was promoted to captain on July 1, 1855. In December Colonel Craig notified him that he was being assigned to Kennebec Arsenal in Maine the following spring. The idea of moving north before another Alabama summer set in was a pleasing one for the Gorgases and helped assuage the inevitable pangs that came from the thought of leaving their first home. They were expecting another child, and on March 17, 1856, their first daughter, Jessie, was born. In late May, Josiah's final orders arrived, but his replacement was delayed in coming, and the family had to endure several weeks of heat before leaving for Maine on the seventh of July.

6

LIFE IN MAINE

KENNEBEC ARSENAL WAS situated on the banks of the Kennebec River in Maine's capital city of Augusta. Adjacent to the Arsenal grounds was the State Asylum for the Insane, and across the river was the imposing state house designed by Charles Bulfinch and built of Maine's white granite.

Amelia was prepared to enjoy her stay in this new environment despite the obvious differences from the way of life in the Deep South. Her associations with Northerners had been happy ones, beginning with Dr. and Mrs. Alva Woods, and including two close friends in Mobile—Marian Dexter, now living in Boston, and Adelaide Bell, who had recently moved back to her native New York. Amelia's stay in the nation's capital eight years earlier had further stimulated her interest in all parts of her country. Another advantage was the fact that a home in New England would give her an opportunity to meet her husband's family and friends. She must have considered that this was only fair, for had Josiah not become so attached to all her relatives while he was stationed at Mount Vernon, he might well have felt overwhelmed by them.

Maine's political climate must have demanded as drastic an adjustment from the Gorgases as the physical climate did. The state had traditionally been Democratic in the years following its separation from Massachusetts in 1820, but with the election of Franklin Pierce in 1852, sentiments shifted, for Pierce, who appointed Jefferson Davis his secretary of war, was perceived as a Southern sympathizer. By the time the Gorgases arrived in Maine the Republican party was in control in the state. In the fall elections Hannibal Hamlin, characterized by Gorgas as a "Black Republican," was chosen governor. Amelia accompanied her husband to the inauguration of Governor Hamlin on January 8, 1857, and subsequently Josiah wrote, "The message delivered afterward by the Governor, he read from the Speaker's Desk. It was not quite as *rabid* and ultra as his stump speeches were, but he declared the South to be a despotism and as such 'aggressive,' and if we did not oppose its encroachments our descendents *would be slaves* and would *deserve to be.*" Later in the winter the Gorgases entertained the Hamlins at dinner and formed a "very pleasing impression of both the Governor and his wife" in spite of political differences.[1]

Josiah spent much of his time at Kennebec, as he had at Mount Vernon, supervising repairs to the Arsenal. The river walls received long-needed attention. Of much greater importance to his wife, however, was the construction of a new kitchen for the commanding officer's quarters.

Both Amelia and Josiah were soon enjoying the social life of the community. They frequently attended lectures and dramatic readings, popular forms of entertainment at the time, and they invited small groups of friends for dinner or supper whenever they felt the family budget could stand the strain. Josiah enjoyed an occasional game of whist, which he called "one of the very best schools for acquiring command of one's temper," and he and Amelia continued to find reading aloud a pleasant pastime for quiet evenings at home.

The Gorgases' greatest joy during this period was their children. On January 1, 1857, Josiah began a journal that he said was dedicated to his children and devoted to their "gratification and instruction." In it he recorded family news and comments on world events but seldom anything about his work. Willie at two-and-a-half was, according to his father a "very bright, quite grave and tolerably mischievous and troublesome little boy." Jessie, he noted on her first birthday, was "a nice plump lovely little thing that gives us the greatest pleasure. We are blessed with fine children certainly."

Although Amelia was devoted to her small son and daughter, she was delighted to share their care with a young Irish woman who came to live with them. Anne Kavanaugh had come to America to marry her childhood sweetheart, who was working in Maine. He was killed in an accident shortly before her arrival, and the penniless girl was forced to find work to support herself. Sent to the Gorgases by a Catholic priest, Anne soon endeared herself to the children as their Nana and relieved Amelia of much of the housekeeping as well as the nursing.

When Congress passed a bill increasing the pay of army personnel, the Gorgases indulged in a little wishful thinking about buying a plantation "when we shall have grown rich." "Such a life would suit Amelia admirably," wrote her husband: "I think she would be quite happy if she could see herself twelve or fifteen years hence the mistress of a hundred bales of cotton per annum and forty or fifty ebony faces, whom she would make happy. She has eminently the faculty of making dependents contented, and would, I dare say, spoil every darkey about her for the use of everyone but herself."[2]

The summer of 1857 found Amelia playing hostess to a number of visitors including Josiah's sister Sarah Dorsheimer and his brother Solomon, who brought with him his daughter Nellie. First to arrive was Dick Gayle, who had recently been to and from Europe as commander of a merchant ship. From Sicily, Dick brought his small nephew a donkey that proved to be tame and gentle and an excellent playmate for the children. His gift to Amelia and Josiah was an oil copy of Guido Reni's painting called *Beatrice Cenci*. Dick spent a pleasant ten days with his relatives, and Amelia saw to it that he met the eligible young ladies of Augusta.

Having acquired a "span of horses," the family drove out regularly in the afternoon. Amelia was expecting her third child and considered the drives beneficial to her "present situation." In the evenings she and Josiah, when not entertaining guests, read Dickens' latest novel *Little Dorrit*, which they found "but poor excitement—a great falling off from the books which gave him fame."[3]

The family was saddened by the death of Mary and Hugh Aiken's two-year-old daughter Nannie Kerr on July 17, 1857. In the autumn Mary, who was terribly depressed over her loss, was persuaded to come to Augusta to be with Amelia when the new Gorgas baby arrived. A second daughter was born on October 28 and named Mary Gayle for her aunt. With Mary's help Amelia recovered quickly, though Mary wrote her husband that as oppressed with grief as she was, she had not been very good company for her sister.[4]

While Mary was still in Augusta, word came that Josiah would probably be ordered to Charleston Arsenal in South Carolina. Because Hugh Aiken was planning to set up a business there, the two sisters began happily making plans for joint housekeeping arrangements. Before Mary returned to South Carolina at the end of November, Jessie and the infant Mary Gayle were christened by the Episcopal minister, Mary Aiken acting as godmother for her namesake.

The early months of 1858 passed without word of the new orders. Josiah knew that it would cause "real grief" to both Amelia and Mary if he did not receive them. His own feelings on the subject were mixed because he could not help questioning the advisability of uprooting his family so soon again, though he understood the definite advantages, among them the milder climate and the availability of domestic help. In April Anne Kavanaugh informed the Gorgases that she would have to leave them to join her brother in Portland. This news was a real blow to Amelia, who had come to depend on Anne and hated to think of little Jessie's distress at losing her beloved "Nana."

By the time orders to Charleston finally arrived early in May, Willie had developed typhoid fever. Josiah wrote Colonel Craig that his son's illness would mean a delay in his departure and offered to give up the assignment, but Craig was sympathetic and told Josiah to notify the commanding officer in Charleston of his expected date of arrival. As soon as Willie was well enough, the family moved into the Stanley House, a hotel just across the river from the Arsenal. They expected to leave in a few days and sent their belongings ahead to Charleston, but then Amelia, too, fell ill, and it was decided that Josiah should go on alone and return for the family at the end of the summer, when, they hoped, all would be completely restored to health.

With a "heavy heart" Josiah left his family.[5] He and Amelia dreaded the separation, for they had grown very dependent on each other. Letters back and forth were frequent—Amelia said that writing to him gave her "a world of comfort." Her letters were full of the children's activities and accounts of visits from friends who, she said, did not neglect her. She told him of evening drives with his replacement, a young lieutenant, and the latter's mother, reporting with the frankness that characterized her relationship with her husband, "Entre nous, I have no very exalted opinion of the young gents in-

tellectual attainments but think him kind hearted and well meaning." Josiah apparently expressed concern that her many visitors
were retarding her recovery, but she reassured him: "Company you
know is positively necessary to my existence when you are away."
On rainy days, when she often found herself alone, she accomplished "prodigies of work" on her "fascinating sewing machine."
Amelia passed on to her husband several expressions of regret over
his departure. One man, she noted, "is eloquent in your praises &
says your like never will be seen here again & never has been since
Colonel_____'s time.... The sincere regret of these people is I
confess gratifying to me."[6]

Both Josiah's sister, Eliza Chapman, and Adelaide Bell asked
Amelia and her children to visit them that summer, but she refused
all invitations, feeling that she should remain quietly where she was.
From Mobile had come the distressing news that Judge Gayle was
suffering from cancer, and she deeply regretted her inability to go to
him. She hoped that a visit would be possible once she had settled
her family in Charleston.

The Aikens joined Josiah in Charleston early in June, and Mary
took over the housekeeping at the Arsenal quarters. Josiah wrote
Amelia that everyone in the city went out driving "toward sun-
down," adding "I am quite prepared to break myself on a nice turn
out—stylish horse and a neat carriage. Mary is quite particular & I
think felt quite put out at driving to the Depot in the Ordnance
buggy—which is not *too* genteel—& a trunk is behind!" Amelia's
reply was, "I don't know whether I approve of all that pride of
equipage, I'd rather spend the money on agreeable entertainments
but the majority rules of course." She wanted very much for Josiah
to be happy in Charleston: "I know dear Jesse that you are there
solely for my sake ... so I really feel responsible for your content-
ment and happiness—what will I not do for you darling in compensa-
tion for so many sacrifices?"[7]

Mary Aiken was able to send Amelia first-hand news of their
father when she and Hugh visited him in Mobile in July. She wrote
that in the face of terrible suffering, his patience exceeded anything
one could imagine.[8] When Hugh returned to South Carolina, Mary
remained in Alabama, hoping to relieve her stepmother of some of
the burdens of housekeeping.

Sending daguerreotypes of the children to their father by a friend
who was traveling to Charleston, Amelia wrote, "My homely phiz I
cannot consent to give you dearest." Josiah stood the children's pictures up in a row on the mantelpiece to enjoy them, writing Amelia
that four-year-old Willie was "certainly a fine looking little fellow."
Amelia mentioned that Willie wanted to go out as soon as he was
dressed in the morning and that he was happy in the depot handling
freight and turning the handcar. The depot was just across the street
from the Stanley House, and the station master was undoubtedly a
very patient man. Amelia also told her husband that the donkey
Uncle Dick had given Willie was doing "brave duty" and relieved
her almost as much as another nurse.

There was great joy when the children's devoted Nana paid them
a surprise visit. Amelia reported that "the good soul could not remain longer without seeing her beloved little charges. Poor little
Jessie looked so happy in her Nana's arms that it seemed a shame to
separate them. After many tears and promises to come back, she
returned this morning to Portland. Jessie has been crying all day for
her & her Mamma half inclined to follow her example." Anne kept
her promise to come back, and before the Gorgases left for Charleston had agreed to accompany them on a more or less permanent
basis.

As the weeks passed both Josiah and Amelia found their separation more and more trying. "Oh Jesse I never will consent to be
separated again no matter what the necessity may be," wrote
Amelia. "I am constantly thinking of you—longing for you and my
little pets—There is no peace or happiness away from you for a quiet
man like myself," responded her devoted husband. He understood
the anxiety she felt for her father and wrote her:

> I now think it is strange what an attraction he exercises toward even
> me—a stranger to his blood. But I owe him "Heaven's best gift"—my
> darling wife—and he is associated with all the happiest periods of my
> life—our courtship—our wedding—& the birth of our two babies—
> what events! Talk of battles, politics, travels! A man has no experi-
> ences worth mentioning until he loves the woman he weds & has
> children born to him by her.[9]

Amelia continued to take a lively interest in matters involved with her husband's work. The Army Appropriations Bill passed by Congress in mid June had included $2000 for bringing gas to the grounds of Kennebec Arsenal and funds for proceeding with the work Gorgas had started on the retaining wall. She wrote him that a friend had told her that Congress had passed "your gas bill." The secretary of war would not sanction it, she reported, "but Mr. J. Davis told Mr. Fessenden he knew you & if you recommended it & he, Mr. F. desired it—[10]the bill should pass in spite of the Sec. for he was sure you would suggest nothing that was not proper—See how well you stand at headquarters—The citizens of Augusta are enchanted & are ready to petition for your return that the appropriations may be expended judiciously."[11]

Undoubtedly pleased by these expressions of esteem, Josiah wrote Colonel Craig in early July asking for leave to return to Maine for his family. He mentioned that he wanted to bring them slowly south, stopping at Old Point Comfort on the way. Apparently, this request did not sit well with Gorgas's superior, for his application was disapproved. Josiah was hurt and disappointed, pointing out that he had "had no leave of absence for six years."[12] Amelia was concerned too: "I think of nothing but your leave & the possibility of delay—if Mr. Jeff Davis were only sec. I would take a trip to Portland to see them. How did you like his serenade speech—I thought it very apropos and graceful."[13] (Davis, who was vacationing in Maine with his wife and two children, had been honored by its citizens with a serenade shortly after his arrival, and had replied with an impromptu speech that received wide notice in the press.)

Gorgas wrote Craig that if he could not have a sixty-day leave he was willing to take what he could get—"forty, thirty, or even twenty days."[14] On July 17 he wrote Amelia that the colonel had again declined to grant his request: "I do not know what will be the upshot of it." Amelia was even more disturbed and responded:

> What does the Col. mean by refusing your second application? He certainly has some good reason for denying what is absolutely your right—then too you have generally been treated remarkably well by the old fellow which renders me doubly anxious as to this queer

conduct—I am bitterly disappointed but don't do anything rash—If you cannot come on for us, I can join you without the slightest difficulty—Willie and Jessie are so easily amused they are no trouble traveling & Mamie is a little model of goodness. You know the journey from here to N. Y. is direct & through by daylight & from there we could take a steamer.... If you prefer I will meet you at Old Point.... Make any arrangements you think best dear Jesse & I will cheerfully accede—only try & not lengthen our separation.[15]

Amelia's maturity at this point is evidenced by her desire that her husband do nothing "rash," in other words, nothing that would jeopardize his career, and by her obvious willingness to make the trip south alone with the children in spite of the difficulties such a trip would involve.

Eventually Josiah received permission to go north for his family, his short leave to take effect when an ordnance sergeant should arrive in Charleston from another base. "Heaven knows when that will be," wrote Josiah, but on August 7, he was able to leave, arriving in Augusta four days later.[16]

Traveling slowly south, the Gorgases reached Philadelphia on August 25 and learned with alarm that an outbreak of yellow fever in Charleston was reaching epidemic proportions. Knowing as they did the dreadful effects of the disease, they decided that Josiah should ask for an extension of his leave. Before Colonel Craig could reply, fate intervened in the person of the secretary of war, Dr. William Crawford's old friend, John Buchanan Floyd, who happened to be traveling with the Gorgases on the train between Philadelphia and Baltimore. Hearing of their fears, he granted Josiah verbal extension of his leave and assigned him to temporary duty at Fort Monroe.[17]

7

JOY AND SORROW

THE GORGAS FAMILY STAYED in Virginia until early November, and it was a pleasant time for all of them. As long as there were summer guests at the Hygeia Hotel at Old Point Comfort, they remained and enjoyed the society. Later they moved over to quarters at the Arsenal, making do with the simplest housekeeping arrangements and continuing to delight in the pleasures of the seaside. Nurse Anne and the children were especially reluctant to move on, but Amelia was eager to get to her new home. Mary had returned to Charleston from Mobile and reported the Arsenal quarters freshly painted and in readiness for their arrival. Amelia was probably relieved to have this particular news, for during the summer she had written Josiah, "If repairs are to be made cannot the work be finished this summer? I confess a terror of being turned out of our kitchen again."[1]

Quickly making herself at home in any society in which she found herself, Amelia thought Charleston was particularly agreeable. There she discovered an old friend in Mrs. Robert Barnwell Rhett, a schoolmate at Columbia Female Academy.[2] Mrs. Rhett's husband was editor of the Charleston *Mercury* and a leading voice for secession. (The extremes of political feeling in the country could hardly have been more dramatically impressed on the Gorgases than by the contrast between the vehement abolitionist sentiments expressed by Hannibal Hamlin and the fiery secessionist views of Rhett.)

Amelia was happy to be back in the South, though another pregnancy prevented her from going to Mobile to see her father, whose health continued to decline. Josiah indulged in his favorite pastime of cultivating fruits and vegetables, "helped" by Willie, who received gardening tools for Christmas. By April they were picking their own strawberries, and Josiah began work on a project to erect a fountain on the grounds with a windmill to pump the water for it. He had a donkey cart made for the children's pleasure.

In May *Russell's Magazine* began the publication of the series of letters written by Josiah and his friend John Hillhouse during the months just following Josiah and Amelia's marriage. Josiah said that he placed little stress on the literary merit of the work, "Epistolary Gossipings of Travel, and Its Reminiscences," but "as the Editor desires to publish,[3] we are quite willing to contribute them for the sake of preserving them in printed form." The twenty-two letters, printed anonymously, were full of wit, humor, and literary allusion.

On June 4 the Gorgases became the parents of another daughter, but some weeks passed before they decided on her name. Josiah noted, "Her mama hesitates to call her after herself (as I wish) or after Mrs. Dexter (Marian) or Mrs. Bell (Adelaide). As they are all good names, which is what I bargain for, I await her decision without impatience." To his great satisfaction, the child was named Christine Amelia for her mother and for her father's sister, Christine Zerbe of Cleveland, Ohio. The baby was soon called simply Minnie, her father's nickname for her mother. At first she did not thrive, and in July a black wet nurse was secured for her. She was soon "as plump and lovely a little baby as need be."

On the twenty-first of July Judge Gayle died in Mobile. "Amelia was overcome with grief and wept as if her heart would break," wrote her husband, who had continued to hope that he could take her to see her father before the end came. The tributes paid John Gayle by the Mobile press and by his associates of the Mobile Bar helped to console his family. Josiah, who had the greatest respect and affection for his father-in-law, said, "He was a man beloved and respected by all who came in contact with him—a pure, conscientious, upright man, whose memory deserves to be cherished and his life imitated by his descendants."

In August the Gorgases took a house on Sullivan's Island, one of the favorite resorts of Charlestonians, and remained there until October. They returned to the Arsenal in time for Amelia to be with her sister Mary when she gave birth to a son, John Gayle, on October 16. This occasion was cause for great rejoicing, for, as Josiah wrote in his *Journal*, the mother's heart "had been dead to almost every joy since the death of her little girl" two years earlier.[4] The infant was christened with his cousin Minnie Gorgas the following spring.

National events were moving inexorably in a direction that was to bring an end to the comfortable family life of the Gorgases and the Aikens. In his *Journal* Josiah described the hanging of John Brown in December 1859, and he followed closely the action of the National Democratic Convention held in Charleston in April 1860. The Gorgas quarters at the Arsenal were filled with friends who had come to attend. Josiah's journal entry for April 25 reads:

> Went to see the Democratic Convention yesterday; it is sufficiently boisterous. The President, Hon. Caleb Cushing has trouble enough to keep order, tho' a man of commanding ability and great experience. . . . It is believed that if Mr. Douglas is nominated the Gulf States have arranged to leave the Convention. Then "farewell content." A happy issue will, however, I dare say, be found to all their political antagonism.

Josiah proved a poor prophet. The convention did *not* find a "happy issue"; and after thirty of the Southern delegates had withdrawn and organized separately, the convention adjourned with plans to meet again in Baltimore in June.

Early in June Josiah received word that he was being ordered to Frankfort Arsenal in Philadelphia. This post was more important than any other he had occupied, and he later found that his assignment there was due in large part to his friend Secretary Floyd. In spite of his satisfaction over the new post, he recorded his misgivings about moving again, saying that he found the constant breaking of ties more and more disagreeable:

> I do not want Willie to take or retain a commission in the Army. My great regret is the wandering life we are obliged to lead; this will be the fifth post we have occupied since our marriage. I dislike to part with things, especially growing things, which I have collected about me, and I continually fancy how happy I could be with a spot of earth which I could call my own, which I could plant and improve; where the same things would be constantly about me; where I could live and die and where some of my children might live and die after me.[5]

While Amelia undoubtedly shared these sentiments with her husband, probably the breaking of ties with friends was hardest for her. Amelia found people more fascinating than places and things.

On July 9 the Gorgases said goodbye to Charleston and, accompanied by Mary, Hugh, and little Gayle Aiken, took a night train for Columbia. Early the next morning they drove around the wide dusty streets of the town to see the beautiful new capitol, which was still under construction, and South Carolina College, where John Gayle had been educated. They parted from the Aikens at Winnsboro, proceeding by train and steamer to Philadelphia. The journey concluded with a wagon ride—which the children must have enjoyed—from the depot to Frankfort Arsenal overlooking the Delaware River.

The Gorgases were to remain at Frankfort Arsenal only nine months. Josiah was particularly pleased by his appointment to the Ordnance Board, which studied new inventions and recommended changes for the Ordnance Service. His interest in experimenting with and improving equipment dated back to his duty at Fort Monroe before his marriage.

During these months at Frankfort Amelia and Josiah faced together the crisis that was dividing their country. Abraham Lincoln was elected president on a ticket that Josiah called "purely sectional."[6] South Carolina seceded, followed quickly by Alabama, Georgia, Florida, Mississippi, Louisiana, and Texas. In February 1861 Jefferson Davis was elected president of the government formed by the secessionist states. Soon afterwards Captain Gorgas was offered a commission as major to be detailed to ordnance duty in the Confederacy's corps of artillery. At first he turned down the offer. "All my sympathies are with you," he wrote General P. G. T. Beauregard on March 10, but he added, "with renewed prospects of a peaceful separation I hope there will be the less necessity for haste."[7] Soon thereafter, however, he was ordered to leave Frankfort Arsenal for foundry duty. He felt this an unfair assignment coming so soon after his last move and decided to "make one move of it and go where I should ultimately have to go, I doubt not." He sent in his resignation on March 27 and made plans to report to Confederate Secretary of War Leroy Pope Walker in Montgomery early in April. He would leave his family in Charleston on the way south.

The momentous decision to resign his commission in the United States Army was not made overnight, but rather as the result of a sequence of events. Had he married another woman, the decision of this officer from Pennsylvania might have been a different one; but Amelia did not advise her husband, who said that he was urged on by his "own sympathies and likings."[8] Amelia knew that the choice had to be his, and she was prepared to accept whatever he decided. That he chose to cast his lot with her beloved South made it easy for her.

WARTIME RICHMOND

WHILE JOSIAH BEGAN his work as chief of ordnance for the Confederate government, Amelia, the children, and Anne Kavanaugh settled down in Charleston to await the arrival in August of yet another addition to the Gorgas family. They had not been there long when the bombardment of Fort Sumter began. Sitting at their window listening to the guns, Willie said, "Mother isn't it solemn?"[1] Just how solemn it was, Amelia must have realized, for war now seemed inevitable, and her husband was faced with the awesome responsibility of supplying the struggling new government with arms and ammunition.

When the headquarters of the Confederate government were moved to Richmond in May 1861, Josiah decided to establish the main ordnance office in the Virginia Armory situated at the foot of Fifth Street between the Kanawha Canal and the James River. It was not far from the Tredegar Iron Works, which were to produce many of the weapons used by the Confederate army. Josiah moved temporarily into the "newly finished and elegantly furnished" Spotswood Hotel, where Jefferson Davis and many of his cabinet members were staying.[2] The city soon became a vast training ground for troops; as officers, government officials, and workers began to arrive, living quarters became very scarce.

After much searching, Josiah was able to secure four large rooms with board for his family, which now included Maria Bayne Gorgas, who was born on August 4. He brought Amelia, Anne, and the five children to Richmond in October. The Gorgases would have preferred a house, but they were thankful to be united once more; and, as housekeeping had never been an unmixed blessing in Amelia's eyes, she accepted the arrangement gratefully.

Amelia was welcomed to Virginia by two friends from Mobile days—Mrs. James Alfred Jones,[3] niece of the Gayle's longtime friend, Confederate Senator Francis Strother Lyon, and Mrs. George Wythe Randolph,[4] the wife of Thomas Jefferson's grandson, who served as secretary of war for the Confederacy from March to November 1862. Another wartime resident of Richmond to whom Amelia became devoted was the wife of Josiah's West Point classmate Smith Stansbury; she soon became "Auntie Stansbury" to the children. These women proved themselves true friends when Amelia and all five children were stricken with scarlet fever in December 1861. Mary Jones wrote to Sarah Crawford, who was still living in Mobile:

> Miss Amelia desires me to write to you as she fears you may be uneasy at her silence.
>
> You have heard how very ill Jessie and Mamie were last week with scarlet fever. I am very glad to tell you that they are both well enough to be up and dressed today. Willie, the baby, and Minnie had it very slightly. At one time I thought Jessie and Mamie in great danger—now the only care will be to guard against cold. I feel confident this will be done.
>
> The very night Jessie and Mamie were considered out of danger, Miss Amelia was taken sick. At first we thought it nurse's sore throat but Saturday the eruption peculiar to scarlet fever made its appearance. She is very sick today but the Dr. thinks if we give her stimulants regularly through the night she will be better tomorrow. She was so worn out nursing the children her debility is very great. At first her throat gave her most trouble but now she suffers principally with nausea. She has most attentive nurses in Mrs. Stansbury and Mrs. Randolph, the former has staid every night with her since the children were thought very sick. Dr. Smith, her physician is an excellent one, so you may rest assured she has every attention. If Miss Amelia should become worse, we will telegraph you, but if you don't hear until this reaches you, you may feel satisfied she is better. I will write constantly and keep you advised of her situation.
>
> This morning Willie woke up with the measles broken out all over him; as none of the children have had it, I suppose it will take the rounds.

As I haven't time to write to Maria, please let her know of Miss
Amelia's sickness. I am writing from her room. Mrs. Randolph is near
me and says she thinks she is a little better than she was this morning.
I will write again tomorrow or next day—until then good-bye.[5]

When Amelia and the children had recovered and settled down
into as normal a routine as the times permitted, Amelia was able to
take part in the Richmond ladies' activities designed to further the
war effort. Young and old had taken up knitting, and sewing
machines were kept busy. The machine Amelia had bought in
Maine became an even more treasured possession in wartime
Richmond. Thousands of sandbags made by the ladies were sent to
General John Bankhead Magruder for the defense of Yorktown.[6]

The women organized the Ladies Defense Association to raise
funds for the war effort and in general to coordinate the women's
activities. Mrs. Randolph was the able president of the group. One
of its major tasks was to secure for the hospitals necessary drugs that
often had to be smuggled in from the North.

The winter of 1862 brought days and weeks of snow, rain, hail,
and sleet. Heavy rain fell on the inaugural ceremonies on February
22 when Jefferson Davis was sworn in as president of the Confederate States. The gloomy weather reflected the fate of Southern armies
on the battlefield. With the rest of Richmond the Gorgases lamented
the fall of Roanoke Island, Fort Henry, and Fort Donelson. Gone
were the high hopes that had followed the Battle of Manassas the
summer before. The Battle of Shiloh in April brought even greater
concern to Amelia, whose brother-in-law Thomas Bayne was
wounded there. Fortunately, he recovered soon enough to move his
family out of New Orleans before it fell on April 25.

Richmond's defenses, too, were being challenged, and President
Davis decided to send his family away from the city. Before they
left, he decided to join the Episcopal Church, of which his wife was
already a member. The Reverend Charles Minnegerode, rector of
St. Paul's Church, which they attended, arranged a special confirmation service and wrote Amelia of the plans:

Although it's not my intention to spread the news of it before
hand—I feel it my duty to let *you* know in the hope that you & (oh

how I wish it) your husband, may embrace the same opportunity. I would be so glad if you could look upon this as a providential call and obey it. I would prefer it to have him [the President] confirmed with several others. One young lady I think will certainly join in it. And how rejoiced I would be to see you there too & still more so if joined by your husband.

Always drawn to the Episcopal Church in which she had been married, Amelia had never formally joined it. She apparently welcomed this opportunity—Mr. Minnegerode had written, "your mind *is* made up."[7] Josiah agreed to take the step with her, and they were both confirmed with President Davis at a noontime service on May 6, 1862. The preceding Christmas Josiah had given Amelia a copy of the *Book of Common Prayer* inscribed "Amelia R. Gorgas, Richmond, Va./Christmas 1861/from her husband/J. G."[8]

Richmond breathed more easily after Federal gunboats were forced to turn back below Drewry's Bluff in mid-May and after General Joseph E. Johnston's forces had fought General George B. McClellan's divisions to a standstill at Seven Pines on May 31 and June 1. Nevertheless, Josiah concluded that his family would be safer away from the city during the summer and arranged for Amelia, Anne Kavanaugh, Mrs. Stansbury, and the Gorgas children to join a group of forty or fifty "refugees" at a Methodist college in Greensboro, North Carolina.[9] Willie went on to Winnsboro, South Carolina, to visit his aunts Mary Aiken and Maria Bayne and their families.

Tom Bayne had joined Josiah in Richmond after leaving his family in Winnsboro; he became a captain of artillery for ordnance and his brother-in-law's invaluable adjutant. Accompanying Bayne to Richmond was his good friend John A. Campbell, who had resigned his post as associate justice of the United States Supreme Court to cast his lot with the Confederacy. General George Wythe Randolph asked him to serve as assistant secretary of war, a post he would hold throughout the war.[10]

In close touch by mail during the summer, Amelia and Josiah often lamented that once more such a separation had become necessary. He kept her informed about the fighting around Richmond and in early June wrote that he feared he could not take leave to visit the family: "... I dare not ask for what is not absolutely necessary at such an hour. Everyone must be at their post. We hear no news of McClellan's designs. He seems to be lying quietly in his secure resting place, dressing the wounds of his battered army." Later he wrote, "This inevitable business will keep me here steadily. Momentous events are certainly on the eve of happening and if anything in my department were to go wrong it would undo all the good I have done."

General and Mrs. Randolph were good friends to Josiah during Amelia's absence. He wrote her of breakfasting with them at their Franklin Street home one Sunday in August: "... no one there except the English terrier puppy, which is almost as much noticed as a baby ought to be." They did their best to help him find a place for his family to live during the coming winter. Many of his letters to Amelia described his efforts toward this end. He was "astonished" at the prices asked for some accommodations and wrote that their land-lady of the previous winter would not be willing to "undertake" them again. "I fear housekeeping is out of the question and nearly impossible and board quite beyond our means. What will this lead to? Separation for an indefinite time? ... I think you will have to leave all of the children and come to look up quarters for us. I shall never be able to do it."

Another alternative Josiah proposed was that his family could move to the Armory and set up housekeeping there, but he hesitated to press this plan because he feared Amelia would not be satisfied. He knew how much being near her friends meant to her, and al-though the Armory was not far from the fashionable part of town, the approaches to it left something to be desired. Josiah wrote his wife of a chance meeting with Judge Campbell, who was also house-hunting. "The Judge is out of patience. He says the *women* have just such a part of the city they must live in, and just there he can't find a house to buy or rent." Josiah could sympathize with him.

In the end the Armory was decided on, unorthodox as it was for living quarters. Josiah furnished it as comfortably as he could and wrote Amelia that the playgrounds would be "capital and that the children would thrive."[11] His family finally moved into their new home at the end of the year after spending the fall in Winnsboro. Soon the Armory was a gathering place for Gorgas friends and relatives. Tom Bayne made his home with them, and after the birth of his daughter Edith in Winnsboro, he brought Maria and their children to join him. The two families shared the quarters for several months. Willie, now nine years old, was enrolled in Mrs. Munford's school just a few blocks away from the Armory.[12]

Housekeeping became increasingly difficult as the war progressed. Costs were exorbitant. In March 1863 Josiah noted in his journal, "Flour is $30.00 a barrel here, and twice and three times that price elsewhere. The difficulties of transportation add to the scarcity. We now pay three dollars per pound for butter; two dollars for eggs; a turkey costs fifteen dollars; beef is $1.50 per pound; common domestic is two dollars a yard; calicoes are unattainable." In spite of the astronomical costs, he and Amelia were able to entertain small groups of friends from time to time. Their guests were often officers just in from the field who were able to give Josiah and Amelia the latest news from the battle areas. On one such occasion their guests included General Francis A. Shoup, who had recently fought in Arkansas, and Mrs. Lafayette Guild, the wife of General Lee's medical advisor and an Alabamian. On another evening the guest of honor was Dr. W. A. Spotswood, chief of surgery for the Confederacy, who had married Amelia's cousin Mary Eastin. Such social events were a part of life in many Richmond homes during the war, helping to ease the terrible tensions of the days.

Amelia's nursing skills were often called into use during the war years. There was a "fearful" accident at the Ordnance Department's laboratory on Brown's Island in the James River in the spring of 1863. Sixty-nine people, sixty-two of them women or girls, were killed or injured in an explosion. Amelia was "untiring in aiding, visiting, and relieving" the wounded, and Josiah wrote that she had done "an infinite deal of good to these poor people." Hundreds of wounded men were brought to Richmond after· the Battle of Chancellorsville in May, and Amelia went each day to the hospital at the corner of Seventh and Cary streets. Josiah lamented that she could not spend more time from her household duties, for "she is a very apt nurse." One day she amused the family by telling them about a soldier who asked her to smoke his lighted pipe until he could get ready for it.

Shortly before the battle at Chancellorsville the city had been

thrown into a "violent commotion" when news came of a threatened
Union cavalry attack. Josiah wrote in his journal on May 3 that the
people had been in "utter despair":

> Citizens turned out with all sorts of arms and mustered on the
> public square. Senators and Cabinet officers fell into the ranks, and
> were marshalled to the batteries under direction of General Ran-
> dolph. The Yankees came no further, however, but crossed over to
> the Central and finally to the York River Road, and were last heard of
> some ten miles off, making for the Peninsula. . . . So, happily ended
> the cavalry attack on Richmond.

Spirits were raised with news of Lee's victory at Chancellorsville,
but relief was soon tempered with distress over the wounding of
General Jackson. His death a week later was a blow of immeasurable
magnitude to the Confederacy. Josiah took Willie and Jessie to look
at the face of the "great warrior" as he lay in state in the capitol on
May 12. Josiah wrote that "the crowd nearly crushed us. Mama had
to be satisfied with a peep at the door where the coffin lay. . . ." He
noted that the loss of Jackson "would more than counterbalance a
victory ten times as decisive."[13]

During the summer of 1863 the Confederate forces were defeated
at Vicksburg and Gettysburg and were threatened from Yankee
gunboats on the James. With a temporary lull in the fighting in
mid August, the Gorgases were able to escape the Richmond heat on
a ten-day visit to their friend J. P. Holcombe at his home in the
country beyond Lynchburg.[14] It was a welcome respite for the
adults and a new experience for the children, Willie, Minnie, and
Ria, who accompanied their parents. Soon after their return to
Richmond, Amelia and Maria Bayne spent a pleasant day on a boat
trip down the James from Rockett's Landing to Drewry's Bluff.
Mary Boykin Chesnut of South Carolina, who spent much of the
war in Richmond, called Drewry's Bluff "our Gibralter."[15]

General Lee's arrival in Richmond late in August for consultations
with President Davis brought added excitement to the Gorgases.
Willie met him for the first time and sat in his lap, but Josiah
recorded that Willie seemed disappointed—he didn't think Lee

looked "heroic." A social gathering at the Randolphs' home gave Amelia and Maria their chance to meet the general.

Amelia and Josiah needed the memories of such pleasant occasions to carry them through the difficult winter of 1863–1864. News from the battlefields was on the whole bad, food continued scarce, and concern over rampant inflation increased. "The vast over issue of paper money has raised prices to such a pitch as to make the expenses of government enormous. . . . The fear is that a swift national bankruptcy is coming upon us," wrote Josiah at the end of October 1863. A personal blow to the Gorgas and Bayne families was the capture in November of Richard Gayle who had been commander of the Confederate blockade-runner *Cornubia*. His ship had carried critically needed supplies from Bermuda to the Confederacy, and the loss of his ship was an official as well as a family misfortune for Josiah.

In spite of bad news from many quarters, the inhabitants of Richmond continued to carry on some social life. "In the midst of these gigantic wars," Josiah wrote, "people will still amuse themselves."[16] On a snowy day in January he and the Baynes attended an entertainment organized to raise money for soldiers' relief at the home of Senator and Mrs. Thomas J. Semmes. Amelia, who had been ill and confined to bed for several weeks, must have been much interested in their account of the party which was described by Mary Boykin Chesnut:

> Their success was all they could have desired. The play was charming. . . . The female part of the congregation, strictly segregated from the male, were planted all together in rows; and they formed a gay parterre, edged by the men in their black coats and gray uniforms. Towards the back part of the room, the mass of black and gray was solid. On a sofa of state in front of all sat the President and Mrs. Davis. Little Maggie Davis was one of the child actresses. They had a right to be proud of her. . . . She is a handsome creature and she acted her part admirably.[17]

Later in the month Mrs. Randolph gave a benefit party complete with charades and a "picture gallery" posed by the city's most beautiful young women. The program was written "in dainty and humorous verse" by the poet and editor John R. Thompson and "recited by Miss Mary Preston in the graceful drapery of the Muse of Poetry."[18] Amelia decided to attend these festivities. Loving a party as she did, she must have enjoyed the occasion, though the exertion caused a recurrence of her illness.

By March, Amelia was fully recovered and accompanied Josiah and the children to Capitol Square to welcome a thousand returning prisoners of war. Jessie and Minnie each carried a small basket of provisions, and Willie some cold tea for the men. Apparently, the children had adjusted well to their wartime life. Minnie, now five, was something of celebrity. A Richmond paper reported:

> A Steamboat on the Canal—A beautiful little side-wheel steamer, called the "Minnie Gorgas" so named after the daughter of the efficient head of the Ordnance Bureau, has recently been put upon the James River Canal, and in point of appearance and speed presents a lively contrast to the slow moving clumsy looking boats that have heretofore had undisputed sway of this valuable source of communication through some of the most fertile counties in the State. She was built at the Bellona Arsenal and is the property of the Confederate Government.[19]

Minnie was the special pet of Major Cary, commander of the Bellona Arsenal and foundry, and according to her father her airs with him were comical. Major Cary's gift of several wild turkeys provided a welcome addition to the Gorgases' bill of fare the latter part of March, and Josiah commented that it was incomprehensible to him how the poor were able to live. Even cornmeal was selling at thirty dollars a bushel.[20]

9

THE INEVITABLE END

LIFE IN THE ARMORY may have become a little quieter early in April 1864, when the Baynes and their four children moved into a house of their own, prompting Josiah to note in his *Journal*, "Two families can rarely get along without some discontents in one house and it is well that we have quietly broken in two—pleasantly." The home the Baynes rented was a large one, and on several occasions they were able to provide room for sick and wounded soldiers.

Amelia and Josiah joined all Richmond in mourning the death of President and Mrs. Davis's little son, Joe, who was killed when he fell from the porch of his home. Both attended the funeral on Sunday, the first of May, and afterwards Josiah wrote, "The President is very much attached to his children and very caressing toward them, and this is a heavy sorrow to him. Last winter I once saw him take this little fellow off to hear him say his prayers as he went to bed."

The Gorgases shared the apprehension that swept the city on May 11 when General George Meade's army was reported to be rapidly approaching from Ashland. All Josiah's officers and clerks were called out to the city's defenses. After severe fighting in which General J. E. B. Stuart was mortally wounded, residents relaxed a little, but Josiah felt little confidence that the city could remain free very long. "Our enemy is here in very great force and will harass us in every possible way."

During the summer, fighting was general all over Virginia. Hugh Aiken came to Richmond with his regiment (the Sixth South Carolina Cavalry), which had been sent to reinforce the hard-pressed troops already in Virginia. As Union soldiers poured into the state in ever growing numbers, Southern losses multiplied, and Josiah voiced the feeling of many when he said, "Where can we supply such a waste of men? We can hold out in all else."

After Hugh Aiken was wounded at Louisa Court House in June, Mary came up from Winnsboro and brought him to the Gorgases' to recuperate. Amelia was again pregnant and must have welcomed her sister's company during the summer. The weather was warm, and lack of rain increased the food shortage by causing gardens to wither.

Early in August came news of the destruction of the fleet at Mobile and the subsequent surrender of Fort Gaines and Fort Morgan. Amelia was relieved to know that Sarah Crawford and her children were safely settled at Colonel James Crawford's plantation in Greene County. By the end of the month Josiah was asking himself, "Can we hold out much longer?"[1]

Great personal sorrow temporarily eclipsed Amelia's concern over the war when Maria and Tom Bayne's six-year-old son Gayle died on September 7, 1864. She wrote to her niece, Millie Crawford:

> Since my hasty note to your Mother announcing dear little Gayle's death I have been too much indisposed to write, first with a violent attack of neuralgia & then with many aches & pains which still confines me almost entirely to the house. Maria has written your Mother I think a full account of her dear boy's long & painful illness—She begins to think the child had *camp-fever* but his physician does not encourage such an opinion—he adheres to his original opinion of some organic trouble in his stomach. Poor Maria is sadly changed by the affliction & looks so thin & wan as to excite all our sympathies—she bears up with christian fortitude her heart is breaking all the time. She is going to take charge of the infant son of a friend—Mrs. Thomas of N. O.—who died last summer; this will occupy her very much & I hope divert her thoughts in a measure from her trouble. You can not realize what a fine, manly, attractive boy Gayle had grown—He was large for his age, full open forehead, singularly large clear, blue eyes—exquisite complexion—a smile always parting his red lips & showing a row of pearly teeth—He was the most perfectly obedient child I ever saw & the very darling of his Father's heart.
>
> Mr. Bayne wrote that Dr. Turner, Mr. Chalaron who lives in their house,—and Aunt Hetty rode in one carriage to the grave—Mrs. Goldthwaite—Mrs. Jno. G.—Mr. Owen & Ann followed in another—The funeral ceremonies were performed here by the

Catholic Bishop.—Maria will never spend another summer in Richmond she thinks—though her remaining children never looked as well as they do now—Col. Ould[2] told Mr. Gorgas yesterday that arrangements had been made for the exchange of *naval* officers within the next six weeks—so that poor Dick's prospects are once more brightening & we have every hope of seeing him before the very cold weather sets in—I watch with some interest from my chamber windows, the thousands of yankees imprisoned on Belle Isle; they are tolerably comfortable now but I dare say will suffer during the winter in that exposed situation with imperfect tents to protect them—They cannot suffer however as our poor fellows in the Northern prisons are made to do—very few of those returned last week will live to get home their condition too exhausted to bear the journey.

Genl. & Mrs. Randolph leave tomorrow for Liverpool—& thence to the balmy climate of the Mediterranean Islands—Genl. R.'s physicians decide he cannot bear another winter in this climate his lungs already much affected. He looks wretchedly & I feel many misgivings will never return alive to this country—Their departure is a sad loss to us for we have been upon the most intimate terms since my first arrival in Richmond & Mr. Gorgas has no other friend in the city whose society he so much enjoys—Genl. R. is a most valuable man & the country can illy spare his services at this critical time. . . . Our defeats in the valley have depressed the people somewhat, but as Genl. Longstreet relieves Gen. Early confidence & success will soon be restored—Gen. Beauregard is said positively to have gone to the relief of Genl. Hood which I am sure will restore confidence in that army while Gen. Lee renders Richmond perfectly safe from the approaches of Grant—The grand battle for Richmond will take place before winter sets in & we women must pray unceasingly for the success of our brave armies—The children continue perfectly well & give me very little trouble—Jessie & Mamie are almost exactly the same size, while Minnie & Ria might pass for twins, only one is a dark brunette & the other a flaxen haired blonde. Willie is a *big boy* longing for the time he will enter the army—he is on a visit to Mr. Seddon's, the sec of War, little boy who resides about 20 miles in the country—I think he resembles Billy much in character & appearance—while Mamie's miniature might well be mistaken for you—Jessie is like her Father with whom she is the favorite—while Ria is always mistaken for one of Maria's children—poor little Minnie they say inherits my appearance as well as name—Mr. Bayne sent your Mother a photograph of Mamie Bayne taken about two weeks ago—It is an excellent likeness—The child as you see will make a handsome woman—she is one of the most graceful & intelligent little creatures I ever saw—She spends most of her time down here with Jessie & Mamie to whom she is much attached while our large yard gives her ample play-ground—

Mary Jones is still absent in the country imbibing health up in the mountains—Mr. Jones is down for a few days—taking his meals with us—We are very much attached to both Mary & Mr. Jones—& delighted when we can persuade them to visit us— . . . I have written you very hastily dear—fearing every moment to be interrupted it is now quite dark, & I must go down & talk a little with Mr. Jones

Has Clara forgotten me—Love to your dear Mother little Sallie & Uncle James' family—Your letters give me great pleasure & I am sure you will write more frequently now that I go out so little—

I will write your Mother very soon—[3]

Amelia's hope of seeing her brother before winter set in was fulfilled. Richard Gayle and over 100 other naval officers reached Richmond on October 18 after a year's imprisonment at Fort Warren, the federal prison in Boston Harbor. Two weeks later, on November 3, 1864, Amelia presented him with a namesake. Josiah took note of the birth in his journal:

A little boy was born to us at fifteen minutes before six this evening (Thursday). Mother and son doing very well, but these are events involving terrible suffering. I hope it may be the last. Two boys and four girls in a family will do very well. May heaven bless and protect them all and bring them safely to years of maturity. It is a wet miserable evening, and as I sit writing by the blaze of a cheerful wood fire, I sorrow over our soldiers exposed to the slow, cold, penetrating rain. Heaven watch over them too.[4]

There were two other bright spots for the Gorgas family at the end of a year that cast gloom over all supporters of the Confederacy. Josiah's promotion to brigadier general was confirmed by the Confederate Senate in mid-November, and young Richard Haynesworth Gorgas was christened at St. Paul's Church, the site of his parents' confirmation, on December 4. Amelia described the baptism in a long, news-filled letter to her sister Sarah:

Little Richard behaved beautifully this morning & his proud God-Father made all necessary responses with such dignity & solemnity as will satisfy the most strait-laced churchman—Mary Jones stood as God Mother & I hope the dear child will be worthy so sweet a sponsor—The christening was just before the service & the church was completely filled before we were through—In going out my five children filed out in procession after the nurse & baby, altogether making such a long train of young children that Sen. Henry a friend of ours stopped Mr. Bayne & asked how many—Mr. B. replied the 6 all belong to Gorgas—Ah! replied our friend with a sympathizing countenance—I will offer tomorrow a resolution to give him extra pay & rations. You have no idea how little trouble this last baby gives just because Ria is so much older than the other children were at the birth of my babies—Sunday Dec 11th—You will not believe that I actually had not time to finish a letter to you during the whole of last week—Resumption of housekeeping & long morning visits from intimate friends occupies a great deal of time—I am such a gossip that I never refuse a morning friend feeling sure that they will serve me a nice dish of town scandal while enjoying one of Anne's acceptable lunches—An honest confession but nevertheless perfectly true—They tell me dreadful stories of the corruption of Richmond society much of it growing out of the unprotected manner in which hundreds of young girls, writing in the departments are obliged to live—A large portion of them rent rooms, providing their own meals—entertaining company in their apartments at any and all hours—We all know what the result of such unlicensed intercourse between young unmarried people—

I know you were grieved to see the death of Gen. Gracie—His wife had an infant daughter only four days old & the proud father was reviewing his troops and lines preparatory to a visit to the Mother and child when he was struck by the fatal shell—...[5] Of the group of 4 officers 3 were killed & the one remaining severely injured—Such is war—Mrs. Gracie received much sympathy from the citizens & we all feel very tenderly towards the baby whose brave Father never saw or caressed—Mrs. Gracie has numerous relatives in Richmond but I think she will probably return to her Mother being unable to live without her husband's full pay—I received a note from Hugh just before Gen. Hampton's last engagement—he was low spirited poor fellow, & I feel a sort of presentiment that he will not escape unscathed the coming engagements.

There was rapid firing yesterday occasioned by Gen. Longstreet's attack below Chafins Bluff—I have not heard the results but know hundreds of our brave men lie cold & stiff in a snowy winding sheet—A general attack is hourly expected though the weather is deplorable—the melting snow forming a freezing *slush* through which it seems impossible for men to march.

Mary is decidedly better but still so weak and sick, Hugh determines to apply for a furlough as soon as the fight is over—We are very anxious for her to come on to live in Richmond as long as Hugh is in this Army—The air of Winnsboro oppresses her & she never can recover as long as she lives there. Maria begins to look suspiciously pale & thin & does not deny some grounds for my accusations—She seems distressed at the idea of giving birth to another child, feeling that she is doomed to lose them—I think however her condition & prospects will occupy her mind pleasantly in spite of herself—She has not the least care or trouble with her children having an excellent nurse who keeps them in their 3rd story nursery day & night—They are the most blooming children & very sweet & interesting—Maria sometimes speaks of sending Charley & Edith out to Ma when Helen returns & Mamie to you for the summer—that is if she is obliged to remain here during the summer. If Grant only leaves us at peace, I shall claim Millie next summer whether I remain in Richmond or not.

The winter climate is too severe for her. But I am sure a summer would be beneficial & the Armory a right pleasant resort for young people. . . . If we are compelled to leave this city I shall go to Danville or Greensboro N. C. & in either place feel sure I could offer inducements to bring Millie on. Judge Campbell's family resolve to remain here unless absolutely ordered away. . . . They receive a great deal of company in an informal manner & always make a pleasant impression upon their guests. . . . Mrs. President Davis begins to go out a little & receives visitors as usual. She looks well this winter. The President is suffering from a painful attack of neuralgia—a similar attack some years since lost him the sight of one eye & he has reason to fear the effects of this. When he is well he visits on horseback every night— some portions of the Army encouraging & inspiring the men with his confidence & energy. He always appears cheerful but I know suffers painful anxiety during these trying days—Dick left on Thursday for Wilmington having been assigned to the command of the *Stagg*, a fine new Gov. vessel—he is much gratified with his position & left in fine spirits—he will sail in a week or as soon as the moon permits & vows he will never be captured again—The poor fellow's health is completely broken & *I* much fear he cannot stand the hardships of such a life—He gave us fine accounts of his visit to you which was all too short for his pleasure. . . . Can you not find him a nice wife in Eutaw the poor fellow is crazy to be married, & begs us to interest some sweet girl in his cause as he has no time to prosecute an entire courtship— . . .[6]

As the year 1864 closed the fortunes of the Confederacy were at a low ebb indeed. Everyone was "depressed and sombre," though the young people still found moments of gaiety, and there were many marriages. The Gorgases took note of their eleventh wedding anniversary by having a few friends in for an evening of cards and a light supper.

During January there was much speculation as to General William T. Sherman's next move. Savannah had fallen to him in late December. On the sixth Josiah wrote, "No positive news of Sherman's intentions. Indications are that Charleston, too, will be given up— where is this to end? No money in the Treasury—no food to feed Gen. Lee's army—no troops to oppose Gen. Sherman." By January 18, "The prospect is growing darker and darker about us. . . . A distinguished Virginian, Mr. Holcombe, tells us there is a strong disposition among members of Congress to make terms with the enemy on the basis of the old Union, feeling that we cannot carry on the war any longer with hope of success. Wife and I sit talking of going to Mexico to live out there the remnant of our days." A week later he wrote that he had outlived his momentary depression and felt his courage revive when he thought of Lee's brave army, some sixty thousand strong, in front of them: "The attacks of the enemy will now all be directed against that Army. Sherman from the South, Thomas from the West and Grant in front. We must sustain and strengthen this army, that is the business before us."[7]

February brought further bad news. Charleston was evacuated on the seventeenth and Columbia occupied by the Union army on the same day. Sherman continued his advance. On February 27, 1865, in a skirmish near Cheraw, north of Winnsboro, Hugh Aiken was killed. General Sherman had met Mary when he passed through Winnsboro a few days earlier. He mentioned Hugh's death in a letter to a fellow officer, identifying Mary as "a sister of Mrs. General Gorgas of the rebel Ordnance Department." He added, "In her conversation with me she said she supposed her husband would have to 'submit or get killed' and I answered her that such was the case but I hardly thought so soon to be a prophet."[8]

The Gorgases did not receive confirmation of Hugh's death until March 9. Amelia must have shared the feeling her husband expressed in writing on this occasion: ". . . poor Mary! What a life long of sorrow is there. But he died like a gallant soldier on the soil of his native State and defending it against her foe."[9] Mary was left with two children, Gayle, now six, and Carrie, who would not be three until August.

As the Union armies drew closer to Richmond and hopes of saving the city became increasingly dim, the Gorgases and the Baynes debated again and again what they should do when Richmond had to be evacuated. Amelia expressed her willingness to remain there, but Josiah wanted to move the family to Danville in hopes of keeping them with him.

On April 2 the Gorgases attended services at St. Paul's Church as usual and saw President Davis called from his pew to receive word from General Lee that Richmond must be evacuated at once. By one o'clock Josiah had instructions to leave the city that night. Plans to take the family to Danville were quickly abandoned, and Amelia, with the help of Willie, two neighborhood women, and a horse and wagon began to move as many of their belongings as possible to the Baynes' home about a quarter of a mile away. Josiah had to devote himself to the removal of public property from the Arsenal, but he urged his wife to leave their quarters before the enemy entered the city. When he left her at midnight, she was still struggling with her task, and Willie had finally fallen asleep.

Amelia gave a graphic account of the days following the occupation of Richmond in a letter to her brother Dick, who had been made a prisoner of war a second time after the capture of his new ship, *The Stag*, in February:

> Mrs. Gracie leaves tomorrow morning under most favorable circumstances & promises to mail this letter to you, the first written since the evacuation—Mary Jones & I moved up to Maria's Sunday night, the gentlemen leaving us between 12 & 1 o'clock on the last train which we learn reached Danville safely. The federals entered the

city early Monday morning very quietly & preserving excellent order. The burning tobacco communicated fire to adjoining buildings quickly spreading along the canal to the arsenal setting fire to & exploding vast quantities of shells & other ammunition. These laid in waste at least half the city endangering our house & lives. Our front parlour window is shattered by a large fragment shell very nearly striking Mary & Maria who were just leaving the room—Thanks to a Merciful Providence we have escaped all peril unharmed & are comfortably & quietly established we hope for several months at least.

We cannot say too much in commendation of the gentlemanly conduct of the Federal officers promptly affording us protection, & even assistance to those who require it. I have a note from Mr. G. to Gen. Ord,[10] which however I will not deliver unless necessary. Gen Ord is gentlemanly & responds promptly to any reasonable request from a lady. As the wife of an Old Army officer I feel a certain delicacy in asking a favor if I can avoid it. The events of the last few weeks I know have occasioned you great grief & anxiety. The evacuation was painful enough though not unexpected but Gen. Lee's surrender fell like a thunder bolt upon us. I have conversed with many paroled officers of high rank. 4 officers of his staff passed their first evening in Richmond with us & I know from them the act was unavoidable. For three days the brave troops subsisted wholly on parched corn. . . . Gen. Lee thinks you all will be exchanged at once & we have every hope of seeing you in a very short time. News from the South comes slowly. Our gentlemen are with their chief & we pray will continue to follow & sustain him as long as a hope remains. No tidings from poor Mary for several weeks. She bears her affliction better than we could have hoped but continues very delicate. During the occupancy of W. by the enemy, Gen. Sherman called to see her telling her he had dined at our Father's house in Mobile many years ago & remembered him with respect & pleasure. Mary's beauty & dignity commanded respect from all she chanced to meet & I believe saved her house from pillage. I presume bro. Matt is with Ma at Mt. Vernon. It must have fallen with Mobile. Sarah's family were well & comfortable & feel secure under Col. C[rawford]'s kind protection. I have forgotten to say a word concerning our negro servants which would have been a real omission as their conduct is beyond all praise. Mine remain perfectly faithful—indeed never performed their half so well or willingly. Their only trouble is a fear that I cannot afford to keep them, without wages of course, which they all decline receiving from me. Maria is very ailing & expects an addition to her family in July. Mary J. is within a few weeks of her trial & will of course remain with us. Judge Campbell's family are in the city with him—none of them have been molested. Your boy is superb & will amuse you wonderfully with his pretty ways. The children are perfectly well & happy, wholly unconscious of the great changes occurring. If you are exchanged soon as we have reason to hope, try to see Mrs. Gracie in N. Y. Mrs. Dickey will know her address.

Remember me affectionately to our friends if you chance to meet them. Pearl's mother has made us her debtors for life by her kindness to you.[11] Pray write by any & every opportunity. We are very anxious & you are the only member of the family with whom we can communicate. All send much love & your boy a hearty kiss.[12]

Amelia failed to mention in her letter to Dick that she and Willie had probably prevented the Bayne home from catching fire during the burning of the city by placing wet blankets on the roof. She did present the note her husband had left for General Ord at the office of General Godfrey Weitzel, who was in command of the Federal troops in Richmond and was able to secure a guard for their home. The children soon made friends with the guard, who promised them that "next time he would be a nice Confederate and not a bad Yankee."[13]

John Gayle, photograph made in 1928 by his grandson Hugh A. Bayne from a portrait painted about 1835 by an unknown artist *(Courtesy of the William Stanley Hoole Special Collections Library of the Amelia Gayle Gorgas Library of The University of Alabama)*

William Crawford Gorgas in babyhood (*Courtesy of the late Aileen Gorgas Wrightson*)

Captain Josiah Gorgas, soon after his marriage (*Courtesy of Mary Adams Hughes*)

Map of Richmond by W. Eugene Ferslew in 1859. The
star indicates the location of the Virginia State Armory.
(Courtesy of the Virginia State Library)

The Virginia State Armory in Richmond, home of the Gorgas family during the Civil War, from a print by Edward L. Beyer (*Courtesy of the Virginia State Library*)

General Josiah Gorgas, C.S.A. *(Courtesy of the William Stanley Hoole Special Collections Library of the Amelia Gayle Gorgas Library of The University of Alabama)*

The Gorgas home at Sewanee (*Courtesy of the Jessie Ball duPont Library, The University of the South*)

Richard Haynesworth Gorgas, about fourteen years of age (*Courtesy of the William Stanley Hoole Special Collections Library of the Amelia Gayle Gorgas Library of The University of Alabama*)

William Crawford Gorgas at Sewanee, photograph by S. Anderson, Canal Street, New Orleans (*Courtesy of the late Aileen Gorgas Wrightson*)

Josiah Gorgas about the time of his presidency at The University of
Alabama *(Courtesy of the Gorgas Home, The University of Alabama)*

The President's Home, The University of Alabama, 1841 (One of four local scenes, painted in watercolor by Anna Cammer Furman in the 1840s, courtesy of Sara Walls, Tuscaloosa, Alabama, a descendant who owns the originals)

Thomas L. Bayne, Sr. *(Courtesy of the William Stanley Hoole Special Collections Library of the Amelia Gayle Gorgas Library of The University of Alabama)*

Taylor, Jessie, and Minna Palfrey *(Courtesy of George Tait)*

Jessie Palfrey in front of the Gorgas home in Tuscaloosa before the portico was changed (*Courtesy of the late Jessie Palfrey Leake*)

Captain William Crawford Gorgas in 1893 *(Courtesy of Mary Adams Hughes)*

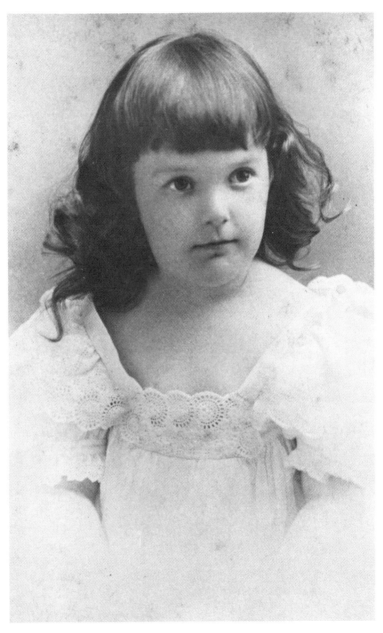

Aileen Gorgas, daughter of William Crawford Gorgas *(Courtesy of the Gorgas Home, The University of Alabama)*

Amelia Gayle Gorgas in June 1905, at the time of commencement exercises when the University alumni presented her with a silver loving cup *(Courtesy of the late Jessie Palfrey Leake)*

Gorgas Home, The University of Alabama, Tuscaloosa, Alabama

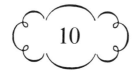

10

A STRUGGLE
AT BRIERFIELD

AMELIA AND MARIA were forced to rely on their own resources and to bear themselves with fortitude as they sought to provide for themselves and their children during the ensuing months. Although Amelia and Josiah wrote each other frequently, letters were slow in reaching their destinations—when they reached them at all. Both women were grateful that their husbands were safely out of Richmond, and they sensibly made the best of the situation.

On May 2 Amelia wrote Sarah, "If we are rendered uncomfortable we will go to some quiet place further north until our husbands decide upon their future. I hope & pray neither of them will return to Richmond. The administration at Washington evidently does not intend to observe Gen. Grant's terms & we can have no faith in their offers of protection to officers returning. Indeed many of the Maryland *paroled* officers have been imprisoned & all refused permission to return to that state."[1] Amelia's fears for her husband's safety were intensified a few days later when their friend Judge Campbell, who had remained in the city, was arrested and imprisoned at Fort Pulaski in Georgia.

After Lee's surrender Josiah and Thomas Bayne had left Danville and traveled slowly south in a wagon, which served them as shelter when they could not find lodging in a farmhouse along the way. They saw President Davis in Charlotte, North Carolina, visited Mary Aiken in Winnsboro, and then secured their paroles in Washington, Georgia, on May 14. Davis had by this time dismissed his cabinet, and the Confederate government was dissolved.

During his stay in Winnsboro Josiah wrote down some of his thoughts on the recent events:

> The calamity which has fallen upon us in the total destruction of our government is of a character so overwhelming that I am as yet unable to comprehend it. I am as one walking in a dream and expecting to awake. I cannot see its consequences nor shape my own course, but am just moving along until I can see my way at some future day.[2]

He reached Alabama at the end of May, but he had no direct word from Amelia until June 14, when he read two of her letters to Sarah. "These," he wrote her, "assure me of your safety and of your preservation from harm during that fearful day which followed the night of the evacuation of the city. They also tell me of the continued health of our dear children and that you are bearing up under the calamities that have overwhelmed us like a good noble woman, as you are, my darling wife." Looking toward the future, Josiah mentioned his hope of devoting himself to some branch of industry if he should be left free to do so. In a postscript he added, "I hope to have a letter from you soon. I don't think there is any necessity for concealment—my whereabouts is quite well known to the authorities and if they desire to arrest me I am on hand." Tom Bayne had left Alabama for New Orleans earlier in June—"the last of my command!" wrote Josiah.

Josiah went on to Greensboro, where Clara Gayle had sought refuge with her children and Amelia's brother Matt, who had broken completely during the war and had to be cared for almost like another child. At the neighboring town of Eutaw, he saw Sarah and her family and reported to Amelia on conditions at Colonel James Crawford's plantation:

> Colonel Crawford has lost 24 of his negro fellows. He takes it as all planters do, philosophically; and would be glad I think if the whole set of darkies could be transplanted to some other clime or country. Emancipation being now inevitable they think the cleaner the riddance the better for the country. It is now a chaotic country—negroes idle and excited—crops but half tilled—no money and no prospects before the planter—He is helpless, tho' entirely convinced that he has no alternative save compliance with the U. S. Gov't and is willing to do his duty as a good citizen.[3]

At the end of June, Josiah visited Demopolis, Alabama, to discuss business prospects with Francis Strother Lyon. At the same time, Amelia and Maria were coming to the conclusion that they must make new housekeeping arrangements if they were to live on their limited means. The little town of Cambridge on the eastern shore of Maryland provided a haven for them, and Dick Gayle, recently released from his second imprisonment, escorted his sisters, nieces, and nephews from Richmond. Before leaving Richmond, Amelia was able to be with her friend Mary Jones when she gave birth to a daughter, Mary Morris. She wrote Josiah of seeing many of his former officers in Richmond. Among them were Minnie's favorite, Major Cary, who was about to leave for Europe, Josiah's cousin Addison Brenizer, who was now establishing himself in business in Greensboro, North Carolina, and Colonel Willcox Brown, who had very kindly offered her the use of a house in Petersburg. She reported that Mrs. Campbell and her daughter, Henrietta Lay, had gone to Washington hoping to procure the release of Judge Campbell, who was suffering in confinement at Fort Pulaski, and she relayed news from the Randolphs, who were still in Europe. "The Gen's health steadily declines & they will not think of returning before next May. He pines for his poor desolated country." She also told her husband that the newspaper accounts of the harsh treatment inflicted on President Davis fell far short of reality: "The manacles were so heavy that he lay prostrate upon the floor of his cell utterly unable to reach his miserable bed. His conduct was heroic, he submitted to the terrible necessity without flinching or murmuring, preserving the dignity for which he was distinguished." She continued, "Oh! Jesse! I am almost heart broken at the results of our struggle and cannot be reconciled to the inevitable consequences. The sight of a blue coat maddens me as the red scarf of the matador infuriates the bull—not a very elegant comparison but true."

Although she found separation from her husband as painful as it had been earlier in her marriage, his safety was now uppermost in her mind. She urged him not to let his family "embarrass his movements"—to go abroad if he thought it best. She only asked that he write "constantly" saying, "I can be very strong if I know of your well doing—but weak as a baby if ignorant of you—"; Josiah replied that with six children, going abroad was out of the question. "We shall then, if we are allowed to, stay in this country and do the best we can."

Josiah began investigating possibilities for developing some of the Alabama mineral regions. He was assisted in his search by Colonel John W. Mallet, an Englishman and a former professor at the University of Alabama, who had served as chemist and superintendent of laboratories for the Confederate Ordnance Department. Amelia was not optimistic about opportunities in her native state:

> I love my state but dread to reside there while the present status of the negroes remains unsettled—indeed I do not feel as if it were my state or country while we are ground under the heel of Yankee despotism. Unless you have some positive business arrangements for next Fall I prefer remaining in this pretty, quiet Md. village until our future is decided upon. Neither Ma nor Sarah are in a position to receive so large a family as mine . . . so I prefer to remain here unless indeed we can be together in some other place. The society here is composed of the very best families of the state & are as loyal to our cause as we ourselves; living is comparatively cheap, excellent schools, nice little church & I am comfortably settled in a *hotel* which you know is the life of all others I most prefer. My family of 9 persons occupying 3 rooms & the use of a fine large piazza board for $120.00 per month, scarcely more than it cost me a week in Richmond. But understand, darling, that I am more than willing to go to the woods, Blount Springs, Montevallo, or any other desert if your interest or happiness are thereby promoted & we can *only be together*. Let me stay where I am until you decide positively what you must do for our future livelihood & in the meantime do for pity's sake try & make me a visit. The war had no such hardship to me as this long & cruel separation. How very much the children would have amused you this summer. Willie is so companionable & manly & the little girls so affectionate & caressing. We think you & Mr. Bayne would have been perfectly happy here. You acted wisely however in remaining quietly South—otherwise you might have been molested. Judge Campbell's family came down this week to remain until the Judge is released.

By September Josiah was writing to Amelia of several job prospects and saying, "I will take the first I can get for this enforced idleness, combined with the uncertainity of the future to us both make me very despondent." He went to New Orleans to consult with his brother-in-law, Tom Bayne, who was rebuilding his law practice and making plans to bring his family, including a son born that summer in Cambridge, back to the city in the late fall. While Josiah was in New Orleans, he received assurances from General E. R. S. Canby, Federal commander of the area, that he would be able to travel freely to Maryland. He wrote his wife in a more hopeful vein, "I hope you have retained your comfortable hotel quarters and will have a place for me. Your statement of finances is quite satisfactory and does great credit to your learning in that branch."[4]

On October 15 Josiah visited the Bibb Iron Works near Montevallo, Alabama. The place had been named Brierfield by the Confederate colonel who had operated it during the war. Josiah wrote, "I am greatly pleased with this property and will try to organize a company to buy it." The property had been greatly damaged toward the end of the war and needed repairs and new equipment, but Josiah felt that his training and experience fitted him better for this undertaking than for any other that presented itself. Finding that it was going to take a good deal of time to arrange the purchase, even though he had found a group of men willing to form a company to buy the works, he proceeded with his plans to visit his family, hoping to expedite the sale by a visit to Washington on the way.

He arrived in Cambridge on November 2, delighted to find his family looking well, and he noted that "for refugees" the life was not bad. He and Amelia began to make plans for reestablishing their life together. He went to Philadelphia to arrange to have the furniture they had stored there when they left Frankfort Arsenal shipped to Alabama; then he moved his family to the Grant House in Baltimore, where they celebrated Christmas together. Soon afterwards he left for Alabama alone and very reluctantly. "I had hoped we would never again separate but we both agreed that it is best for me to go to prepare a place if we are to stay there [at Brierfield]," he recorded in his journal.[5]

Traveling south by boat, Josiah found himself in the company of Mrs. Clement Clay, who had spent the war years in Richmond while her husband, a prominent Alabamian, had served in the Confederate Senate. Clay was imprisoned at Fort Monroe with Jefferson Davis. Josiah wrote Amelia about this encounter:

She had permission from the President to see her husband. She expected also to see Mr. Davis. . . . She talked long and interestingly and told us of the trip in the cars after Mr. Davis' capture and the scenes on board the steamer at Fort Monroe. She has hearty faith in Mr. Johnson with whom she has had numerous interviews.[6] How well she talks! When we parted in the evening she sent her love to you and I sent messages to Mr. Clay and Mr. Davis. . . . She had no reason to think that Mr. C. was now ill treated; but for the first 3 months of his confinement he had nothing to read but his bible and prayer book! What gratuitous cruelty! She had feared the damp of the casemates would cause a return of the horrible asthma under which he had formerly suffered tortures, which she describes so vividly as to make one shudder. She had of course exhausted her eloquence on Mr. Johnson to effect her husband's release; but motives of profound policy, as he said and as she seemed to believe would defer his release yet awhile. She firmly believes that the President is true to the South and will do all he can to restore her political rights.

Amelia wrote Josiah soon after his departure, "Oh darling, hurry in your preparations to receive us for I have begun mine to join you." She was welcomed in Baltimore by many friends and was frequently entertained there. She wrote Josiah of meeting General and Mrs. Edmund Kirby Smith at a dinner party: "The Gen. expressed great regrets that he did not see you & would have called had he known of your being here. Mrs. S. is quite handsome & agreeable & with her two children returns to her Mother in Lynchburg until the Gen. succeeds in establishing himself in some business."[7]

On January 9, 1866, the company formed to buy the ironworks from the government completed the purchase. There were ten stockholders, including Josiah and Francis Strother Lyon, who was the "active party" in concluding the negotiations. Ten days later Josiah arrived at Brierfield to begin the formidable task of restoring, equipping, and putting the works back into operation. "The expenses of such an establishment are so great that it requires some boldness to undertake it," he commented. However, his family felt no qualms at this point. Amelia wrote:

Such a shout as rose from the group of children assembled to hear the result of the sale was loud & joyous enough to have echoed in your own heart so far away. I shall make my preparations to join you in

March the entire healthfulness of the place removing the only objec-
tion to taking the children South for the summer. I feel dearest that
we will be very happy in our Iron home.... We are so much more
fortunate than scores of our poor Confederates that I cannot feel
sufficiently grateful.

Before Josiah had been engaged in his new occupation a month he
was writing, "I find the charge of these works is likely to be a heavy
one, and gives me great anxiety of mind. I hope as the work pro-
gresses the way will seem clearer." He wrote Amelia:

> I am quietly settled in the house where I hope to be for the next five
> years—that you remember is to be the term of your rustication....
> Dearest, I am really disinclined to bring you here, everything looks so
> ruinous and uninviting. All the trees about have been cut away—the
> cabins are ruinous and the sun will be very hot in summer. I will make
> this house as shady and comfortable as possible but you must be
> prepared for an uninviting home. Eventually we can make it pretty
> enough and by midsummer I hope the works will be in operation and
> things will look more cheerful. It is very slow work to get along here
> and we must have a great deal of patience, I find, in addition to a great
> deal of money. Everything we get costs just double what it did before
> the war and a little over.

In mid-February he wrote her, "I find I have about as difficult a
task as I seemed to have when I first began the Ord. Dept. of the
Conf. States."[8] He continued to daydream about the future, in spite
of his discouragement, whether to keep up Amelia's spirits or his
own he may not have known himself:

> After our five years' probation here, when we shall have grown rich
> our girls will be old enough, two of them, to go to school and we can
> select our residence accordingly. Suppose in Paris for example or
> somewhere else in France! In two or three years Willie can go to Mr.
> Tutwiler,[9] which is only about fifty miles, or to Summerfield near
> Selma where there are also good schools. He can come home every
> Saturday from there—or at least every month.

Amelia was prepared to enter cheerfully into any arrangement her
husband made for her. She tried to calm his doubts and did some
daydreaming of her own:

I feel that we shall never regret the Iron works speculation where
you will make a fortune & regain your health; the children be so
happy & healthy & I perfectly contented to bide the time when we
can afford to introduce our daughters into N. O. society by spending
the winter at one of the charming hotels. Did you ever know a woman
of such perverted tastes!!![10]

Amelia, Anne Kavanaugh, and the children reached Brierfield on
April 12. It was a propitious time for their arrival, for spring foliage
did much to enhance the barren surroundings Josiah had pictured to
Amelia. The trees, which in winter had been bare except for the
mistletoe clinging to their upper branches, were in leaf, pines were
plentiful, and Josiah had planted fruit trees and a vegetable garden.
The creek that ran near the house promised pleasure for the children. There was a fine spring, over which Josiah had placed a spring
house that became Anne's particular charge. The Frankfort furniture had arrived safely from Philadelphia, along with the few furnishings that had escaped the fire in Richmond. Amelia had a gift for
making the simplest things attractive, and the Brierfield house soon
bore the marks of her talent.

Although Josiah had competent assistance from Captain William
M. Polk,[11] who had come to Brierfield with him, and from Colonel
Mallet, who divided his time between New Orleans, where he held a
post as professor in the Medical School,[12] and Brierfield, work progressed so slowly that he became more and more discouraged: "I fear
I cannot accomplish what I desire and what I undertook with the
means at my command." The political situation in the country
added to his worries: "President Johnson seems to give way to the
radicals who have the overwhelming majorities in Congress and the
Southern people will be sacrificed."[13] Amelia was hard put to cheer
her depressed husband, but it was her nature to take one day at a
time and expect the best of the future. There were frequently
visitors to entertain and so much to be done in improving the place
that she had neither inclination nor time for brooding.

In early December 1866 she welcomed her brother Richard Gayle
and his bride, Flora Levy of New Orleans, who spent two weeks at
Brierfield following their marriage. None of the Gorgases had attended the wedding, but Amelia received a full report from her niece

Millie Crawford, who wrote that the bride looked beautiful in her low-necked white dress and wore a handsome pearl pin and earrings. She described her uncle as very pale and agitated and said that he kissed them good-night as if he never expected to see them again.[14]

General Joseph E. Johnston spent a few days at Brierfield while the Richard Gayles were there. Willie shot his first bird during the general's visit, and his excitement over this accomplishment so delighted Johnston that he sent the boy a Christmas present of a powder flask and shot pouch.

Early in the new year Amelia and Josiah decided to send Willie to Greensboro to school. His father reflected on this momentous step in his son's life:

> How my heart yearns toward him; and how glad I would be to shield him from the troubles of life. It makes me understand, and in some measure respect the desire people have to *accumulate* in order that they may leave their children in affluence. It is a natural desire of the parent to protect and watch over the offspring—to *work hard* and bear the brunt of the struggle of life, that the child may be saved the same struggle in some degree.[15]

Life was a struggle for Amelia and Josiah at this particular time. The works were now producing some iron, but it was not selling at a profit, and keeping the business afloat financially was a constant battle. Josiah seems to have worried at times about Amelia's isolation from the lively society that had been a part of her life, even during the worst of the war years, but she never gave any indication that she felt at all deprived. During her first year at Brierfield she did not leave the place, although Josiah urged her to accompany him at least as far as Selma, where he went occasionally on business. She spent many hours of the winter planning a Sunday school for the children in the community and in May opened it in a small building that served as both schoolhouse and church. The Sunday school proved very popular and soon had sixty children attending regularly. A visit from Bishop Richard Hooker Wilmer produced great excitement, and Amelia painstakingly decorated the little meeting place for the occasion. The program continued to thrive, and the Gorgas family kept it going as long as they remained at Brierfield, enlisting the aid of visiting nieces to help with the music in the summers.

By late June 1867 Amelia and Josiah were beginning to come to terms with the probable failure of the business. Josiah wrote in his journal:

> We are heavily in debt, and in the present condition of our country—the South—it is impossible to sell stock or borrow money. This leads us to fear that we may have to sacrifice our property, and perhaps lose all we have invested here. It is a sad termination to all our high hopes in great measure attributable to the total prostration of the country. We could make money now and work ourselves out of debt could we but find a market for our products at any rate which we had a right to calculate on.

During July the furnace was shut down, and the stockholders agreed to dispose of the property as soon as possible, but there was little chance of an immediate sale. Josiah's salary stopped with the closing of the works, and he and Amelia had to discuss "reform in the household."[16]

As the summer advanced, the household became a very large one. Matt Gayle, "Ma," her daughter Helen, and Tom and Maria Bayne with their five children all came to visit. With her customary hospitality Amelia welcomed all of them gladly. She loved to feel that her country home could provide a respite from city life, and the Baynes always saw to it that their presence imposed no added financial burden. All the visitors, grownups and children alike, stood on the Gorgases' back porch with opera glasses to witness an eclipse of the moon on Friday, September 13.

Maria returned to New Orleans in November, taking Willie Gorgas and Helen Gayle to spend the winter with her, while Clara Gayle stayed on at Brierfield to take charge of the education of the other Gorgas children.[17]

As Christmas approached once again, there was little to cheer the Gorgas family. Josiah was deeply depressed by his problems. Selling the works seemed impossible in these "disastrous times," and he noted despondently in his journal:

> As the prospect here at the Works closes I look around for some occupation but find it difficult to decide what to do for a livelihood. We must remain here until this property is disposed of, as my interest

in it is so large that I cannot afford to trust another—else I would resign the Presidency and look for a position elsewhere.

The Baynes, whose affairs were much more prosperous than those of the rest of the family, were unfailingly generous, and Maria brought one bright spot to the holiday season by sending a Christmas box for the Sunday school children. Amelia was delighted, for she had despaired of being able to give them anything. "Everybody is so poor—never was the country in such a state of destitution. There is literally no money in circulation," Josiah recorded.

The spring of 1868 brought little improvement. Colonel Mallet, who had worked closely with Gorgas since 1866, left to assume a professorship at the University of Virginia.[18] Captain Polk had already left to enter medical school. He had married one of the daughters of Francis S. Lyon. Prospective purchasers for the works visited from time to time, but no sale resulted. Josiah's health suffered with the decline in his business fortunes. Only Willie's progress in school in New Orleans seemed to promise hope for the future. Amelia wrote him in May:

> Your proud Father & proud Mother offer their congratulations upon your success this month. To stand first in your class is no mean triumph & certainly more than I hoped for or expected. I hope my child that it is an indication of your future career & that you determine to stand first in whatever pursuit or profession you decide to adopt. I feel very grateful to your dear Aunt and Uncle for the encouragement & assistance they give you in your studies. You will repay them one of these days, will you not? I only received your letter today—it having been in the Montevallo P. O. for several days. Grandma and the children spent an hour Thursday evening in fishing—they were entirely unsuccessful but not discouraged. Ward & Mr. Ormand caught several on Sat. & Ward brought me a fine rabbit yesterday of which I made gumbo today. Several boys were in bathing on Sunday but I fear they will be sick from it—the water is too cold. I will try to engage a good rabbit dog for you before your return & you & Eddie[19] will keep my table supplied. . . .
> Richie says to tell Willie Eddie & Dowski[20] call him Dick the Debble & he must lick them for it.[21]

11

A NEW OPPORTUNITY

EARLY IN JUNE 1868 Josiah heard that he was being considered for a position at the University of the South, which the Episcopal Church was planning to open at Sewanee, Tennessee. Toward the end of the month he received a letter from Bishop William Green of Mississippi, chancellor of the projected university, inviting him to come to Sewanee for an interview about the position of principal or headmaster of the junior department, the first branch of the school to be opened.[1] Josiah went to Tennessee the first week in July and was pleased with what he saw. He accepted the position on the condition that he could postpone taking over his duties until March 1869, six months after the beginning of the first term. He did not feel that he could arrange to leave Brierfield any sooner.

The establishment of the University of the South was the result of the dreams and plans of Bishop W. H. Otey of Tennessee, who had suggested such an institution as early as 1835, and of Bishop Leonidas Polk, who had taken steps to organize a Southern church university in the prosperous years immediately preceding the war. In the summer of 1857 at a meeting on Lookout Mountain a "Declaration of Principles" was adopted and a committee appointed to recommend a site. In November a location on the Cumberland Plateau northwest of Chattanooga was approved, and a large part of the land was donated by the Sewanee Mining Company with the condition that the institution should be in operation within ten years. In 1859 Bishop John Henry Hopkins of Vermont, an able engineer and landscape gardener, "planned locations for the buildings, laid out avenues and drives and embodied his plans in the

Hopkins map." Bishop Polk, Bishop Stephen Elliott of Georgia, and Major George Fairbanks of St. Augustine, Florida, built simple frame cottages on the grounds, and on October 10, 1860, the cornerstone, a large block of reddish-brown variegated Tennessee marble was laid.

When war broke out, the hopes for the University were dashed. The Sewanee property was occupied alternately by troops of the opposing armies. The cornerstone was broken into bits; the few buildings were laid in ashes, and the endowment vanished with the fortunes of the Southerners who had subscribed it.

In September 1865 the Diocese of Tennessee passed a resolution that proved to be "the spark which held the life of the University." It voted to establish a theological training school on the domain of the University of the South and elected trustees to work with the new bishop, Charles Todd Quintard, to carry out this resolution. Bishop Quintard raised funds for the construction of a training school building, named Otey Hall for his predecessor, and erected a home for his own family on the grounds. With little more than faith to build on, the trustees then decided to revive the scheme for a university in spite of the impoverished condition of the South. Bishop Quintard was elected the first vice-chancellor in February 1867.[2]

By the time Josiah made his first visit to Sewanee, several homes had been built there, and Saint Augustine's Chapel had been erected. Bishop Quintard had raised funds in England from friends in the Anglican Church, and the next building completed, Tremlett Hall, bore the name of one of the most generous of these English benefactors, the Reverend F. W. Tremlett of St. Peter's Church, Bellsize Park, London.[3]

Although Josiah spent the summer at Brierfield, he went up to Sewanee for a trustee's meeting in August and again for the opening of school on September 18, 1868. Classes began with only nine students, but more were expected, among them Willie Gorgas, who was studying French, Latin, and arithmetic with his father at home so that he would be prepared to enroll at Sewanee when his father took over his new position.

Josiah continued to work over his furnace and to be discouraged both by it and by the state of affairs in the country. "The result of October elections in the three great states of Pa., Ohio, and Indiana rather depresses us, as all have gone for the radicals despite the confident predictions of the Democrats."[4] He made several trips to Sewanee that winter, but he and Willie did not make their permanent move until the first of July 1869, at which time there were almost fifty students (the school terms were arranged to keep the boys on "the mountain" during the pleasant summer months and give them their vacation during the coldest part of the winter). Even then Josiah left much unfinished business at Brierfield, and Amelia regularly wrote him about problems at the rolling mill, prospects for a sale, taxes, insurance, and other matters that show how thoroughly her husband trusted her judgment in relation to his business affairs. However discouraged Josiah may have been as a result of the Brierfield experience, Amelia retained complete confidence in his abilities and blamed the times for their misfortunes. With some satisfaction she reported to him the contents of a letter from a business partner of his to her stepmother: "Speaking of business—he says he presumes these works will be a total loss to the stockholders—he adds— Hardly any avocation or business has done well for the last two years. . . . At least he is in a condition to sympathize with you. He feels that his [other] losses are the result of bad management but thinks your losses up here could not have been avoided by any reasonable foresight. This is a very comforting view for us & I hope other stockholders entertain the same just views."

From Sewanee Josiah wrote Amelia that he would go to work at once to see about a house and try to forget his past troubles: "I can hardly tell anyone how utterly wretched I have been and how great is the relief." The years at Brierfield, perhaps even more than the war years, had left their mark on Josiah, who was now fifty-one. The old buoyancy and the high hopes for the future were gone. The wealth and advantages he had wanted to give Amelia and the children were dreams of the past. All he asked now was to be able to provide simply for those entrusted to his care. Amelia was pregnant once more and disturbed at the prospect of another mouth to feed, but he reassured her, "Dearest, try to think of your future with philosophy—The little stranger will be welcome to me I assure you. I can scratch as well for 7 as for 6—don't let that add to your discomfort."[5]

The Baynes spent several weeks at Brierfield after Josiah left and insisted on leaving Amelia $150 for their board. While she could certainly use the money, she wrote her husband, "This is a great deal too much but if they return in Oct. I will make it all right."

Amelia hated facing another extended separation from Josiah and wrote in August, "What does the Bishop say about the house? I shall never content myself here after the property is sold & you have no interests to look after. . . .My heart yearns for you & I have no courage to live away from you." Later in the fall in response to one of the several possible living arrangements which Josiah suggested to her, she wrote, "But don't worry about us—we are not turned out yet, nor likely to be as long as we wish to remain,—only our years now are too precious to be parted so many months at a time.[6]

She found comfort in Josiah's reports of Willie's progress:

> . . . Your darling Willie is doing very well and getting good marks in his classes. He is studying Greek, Latin, and algebra and I have also put him into the writing class and into spelling—He also takes singing lessons from a Bishop! tell Anne. Good Bishop Young who is a trained teacher of music instructs the boys every day in the rudiments of music. You should have heard the choral service today—very fine—but I fear like many of us you would prefer the old plain service to which we are accustomed. The Lord's Prayer and the Creed are intoned and the Litany sung (almost). Communion is administered every Sunday. Our Board of Trustees meets on Wednesday—There will be seven Bishops, probably, and about 12 other trustees. I expect to entertain Judge Walker and Mr. Toomer Porter—I heartily wish you were here to help entertain all these grand people—Really they are such a body of men as one might well be proud of.[7] But I was going to talk to you of Willie, a subject more interesting to you than Bishops. He is getting acquainted with the boys and never fags in playing.

On another occasion he wrote:

> You are often inquired after and your coming is looked forward to with interest. Mrs. Fairbanks is prepared to be your best friend. She is tall, dignified and well educated. . . . We are getting along pretty well here—only pretty well—It is difficult to make the boys study amid so many female attractions—This is a feature I must try to correct next year somehow. I am anxious to get better control of their time.

Already Sewanee was becoming a popular place for summer visitors. More homes were being built, and many owners took paying guests. Residents were also encouraged to take student boarders, thus sparing the struggling new school the necessity of building dormitories. Bishop Polk had envisaged a society of cultured people growing up around the University, and his dream was beginning to become a reality.

Josiah was very well satisfied with the faculty that had been assembled. Dr. Robert Dabney, instructor in English literature and metaphysics, had been at Sewanee for the school's opening and had served as headmaster until Josiah's arrival. General Francis A. Shoup, now an Episcopal clergyman, came in the fall of 1869 to teach mathematics and act as chaplain. Dr. John Barnwell Elliott, son of the late Bishop of Georgia, who had been one of the earliest Sewanee settlers, became resident physician and instructor in chemistry. Classical and modern languages were taught by Caskie Harrison, a Virginian who had studied at Cambridge, England, and Francis A. Juny, another clergyman. "We are well off now in all Depts," Josiah wrote his wife; "It is only the accommodations we must now improve."[8]

Amelia suffered a miscarriage the second week in September. Her husband rejoined her at Brierfield for a few days but was back at Sewanee by the fifteenth. He urged Amelia to come there to recuperate, but she felt she should stay where she was. Clara, Helen, and Matt Gayle were still living with her, and Anne Kavanaugh continued her competent supervision of the children and the kitchen.

Prospects for a Sewanee home for the Gorgas family continued maddeningly vague. The board had passed a resolution calling for the erection of a dwelling for the headmaster, but no funds were provided, and Josiah hesitated to proceed until the school's financial position improved. Tuition barely covered the expenses of faculty salaries, and funds for capital improvements were very meager. To remedy the situation, the board had appointed a Florida clergyman to solicit funds in the ten sponsoring dioceses, and Josiah wrote Amelia, "As soon as I hear the steps taken by the Board are producing money, I will venture to get the lumber for our house."[9] He planned to have a dormitory constructed in conjunction with their new home so that Amelia could supplement their income by taking student boarders. She entirely concurred in his decision and urged him not to invest his own money in building a home until the school was established on a firmer financial basis: "No enterprise can succeed without money & I am prepared even for the failure of the University of the South if ample means are not forthcoming. I think I can manage to get along with my quota of boarders," she continued, "but I do not *hanker* after them."

Josiah, still concerned that her life must be very dull, encouraged her to go to Mobile or New Orleans for a visit, but she assured him that she did not desire to go to either city without him and that she did not consider herself buried at Brierfield—"Two trains a day & one at night forms a never ceasing excitement & the rolling mill gives life to the place while my household duties leave me not a moment of time to feel lonely—I am very busy just now overhauling the childrens' last winter's clothes determined on purchasing nothing new if I can avoid it—I mean in the way of dresses. We all gather in the sitting room in the evening, Ma, Helen, and I sewing & chatting until 9 o'clock when Ma & Helen retire to their room & I remain by the nice fire & lamp to read."

She was tempted to leave at once for Sewanee, however, when Josiah wrote in October that Willie had broken his arm: "If I were as rich as Mrs. Vanderbilt I would go right after him though I know you & Dr. Elliott will do everything for him. Still if he has much fever & the fracture proves troublesome you must try & bring him home." Anxious as she was, she tried to be philosophical. "God is merciful & good—else my boy might have been taken up with his young life crushed out of him so I shall not give way to grief & repinings but return thanks for his merciful deliverance." She added thoughtful motherly advice—"Get him some amusing books—or I shall send him some—he likes novels you know & you might borrow some from Mrs. Fairbanks or Dabney."[10]

In November Bishop Wilmer confirmed Jessie and her aunt, Helen Gayle. Josiah wrote his daughter soon afterward:

Your Mother tells me you were confirmed on Thursday last by Bishop Wilmer—I was glad to hear it and hope you will continue to be a faithful worshipper of the Lord! I heartily wish your brother Willie had a little of your devotional spirit about him. I think the life up here will suit you very well and will give you abundant assistance in the spiritual life on which you have entered. Our house, that is to be, will be nearly opposite the Chapel & there are two services every day & Communion every Sunday. I hope under your influence Richard will in time be good enough to wish to join you & go with you to that holy table to which we must all look for ultimate happiness—It is a great comfort to me to think of the step you have taken and to know that you are aware of its importance. I rejoice to think that we may be permitted to go often together to the Holy Communion.

I am very glad, too, that your Aunt Helen is now safe within the fold of our Church. I have always been a little afraid of your Aunt Maria's influence with her; and that that might prevail to make a good Roman Catholic of her. Could we not convert Grandma? We must try as otherwise she will lose all our beautiful & convenient Chapel Services here—we are a coat of many colors—Methodist, Presbyterian, Roman, Episcopalian, and finally a little Hebrew-ish.

Willie has just left me to go up to his room, to get his algebra lesson—he sends you his love & a kiss, he says—and many, many regrets that he is so very poor a correspondent—But he is kept pretty busy with his lessons. You would be amused to see how he gets on with his one hand, especially at table—It will be a long time before he can again use his hand & arm perfectly well.

I hope that pig of yours is getting fat. . . . What with the pig & the big turkey your Mother speaks of I think we shall fare sumptuously on our return. . . .[11]

Josiah and Willie returned to Brierfield when the winter vacation began the end of November, and Willie remained with his mother until the new term began in February 1870, though Josiah had to return earlier. There were 110 boys in residence for the session, and Josiah began to feel more optimistic about the school's prospects. In March he wrote Amelia, "Separation is becoming more and more irksome to both of us, and we have not so many years left that we can throw them away. I will go on and put up a wing containing 4 rooms and a sitting and dining room together. This will just give us what we must have and therefore cannot entertain. I will hereafter act on this plan, since you and especially Anne approve it. Our lot is cleared of underbrush and I have rails enough to fence up the rear part of it, so that I can plant trees this month."

In another letter he told her, "I am getting very impatient to have my family here, feeling more and more that this is to be the business of my life. It will make a charming home for us, you will see—tho' of course a quiet one. . . . Last evening (Friday) all the professors spent an evening here . . . as they walked away in the moonlight I thought what an intelligent set of men they were and how pleasant it will be to have such associates. . . . So that you see how your graces and hospitality may be dispensed. I am very anxious to have you *begin*. I know you will be valued and how proud I will be of you."

On a Saturday evening late in March the gentlemen at University Place met to form what Josiah called "our social or literary or conversational club." Meetings were to be held weekly at the homes of the members with no refreshments except a toddy and a biscuit. At Josiah's suggestion it became known as the E. Q. B. Club, "Ecce quam bonum" being the Latin title of Psalm 133 which begins, "Behold, how good and joyful a thing it is for brethren to dwell together in unity!"[12] After the first session Josiah wrote his wife that she would have to get up a "Sorosis" among the ladies if she wanted to keep up with the gentlemen. Her reply was that she was not at all anxious to get up a "Sorosis" if he would let her sip a little of his "nice apple toddy." "Would you literary gentlemen meet if the 'toddy' failed—," she asked teasingly.

Life went on much as usual at Brierfield in Josiah's absence. Amelia's letters continued to keep him informed of local and family news and of the children's activities. In addition they provide fascinating glimpses into the strong, witty, compassionate woman she was. Josiah asked her opinion on a variety of matters, and she rarely hesitated to express her views candidly. In response to his comments about a plan for feeding the students she wrote, "I like the mess plan famously if we could only get old Mr. ____ of Barrancas memory to keep it for us. These widows in reduced circumstances or widows in any circumstances don't seem to understand the business. . . . I think seriously if the mess arrangement fails, you had better build a kitchen on our lot & let us occupy it until we can build." An amusing postscript to the same letter reads:" 'The Home Journal' & the 'Church Journal' afford much pleasure—thanks to Gen. Shoup—I actually read every line of the N.Y. gossip in the Home Journal this afternoon to cure a toothache!!"

She responded to another letter from her husband, "But what is our Bishop coming to? A throne 25 ft. high & a magnificent vice chancellors robe beside that handsome cross he always wears—next he will aspire to be *our* Pope & we will kiss his toe!!! Seriously he is so much in advance of the age that I fear *sectarians* will pronounce him a little crazed on the high church question—Our new Vicar prepared me for rapid strides in that direction, in sentiments but I am timid concerning the outward forms."[13]

Amelia spent many hours in Brierfield, as she had wherever she had lived, ministering to the poor and the sick. Occasionally she found herself rather overwhelmed by her charitable impulses: "My Confederate widows make me daily visits imploring for some assistance to reach Elyton.[14] After the failure of several plans I conclude to raffle our heifer calf for $15.00 & I accordingly sent to Mr. Starr to get it up for me—He raised the first evening $9.00 many of the men taking two chances—After the departure of these poor women I shall never again take the burthen of a community upon my shoulders—my sympathies are so much enlisted that I sometimes think my health suffers from it—& yet poor creatures I am glad to comfort them."

By May 1870 sufficient progress had been made on the house "wing" and kitchen for Josiah to make plans to move his family to Sewanee in late June. Amelia, whose hair was now snow white, celebrated her forty-fourth birthday before leaving Brierfield. She wrote Josiah about the simple festivities:

> My birthday yesterday was sweetly remembered by our affectionate Jessie who presented me with a little book of poetry called *The Changed Cross*, a vol. she knew I wanted so much, & then she gathered a fine dish of green peas for my dinner & Lucy & Anne added other dishes making quite a birthday repast. My little girls are so careful of my comfort that I am grateful every day for such treasures—my pride and chief jewel though will ever be Willie—my first born.[15]

Josiah arrived at Brierfield on June 18, 1870, and a week later moved his family at long last to their new home at Sewanee.

12

SEWANEE

AMELIA MADE THE MOVE to Sewanee with high expectations. Josiah had given her such a vivid picture of life "on the mountain" in his letters and conversations that she was well prepared to take her place there when the time came. Although she had vigorously denied feeling isolated at Brierfield, she must have been delighted at the prospect of being part of a well-educated, cultivated group of people once again.

The move itself was strenuous, and soon afterwards Amelia became ill with a severe infection that brought her close to death. Fortunately, "the disease took a favorable turn and she recovered as rapidly as the attack had been sudden."[1] The family's cramped quarters in their dormitory wing did prevent Amelia's doing any extensive entertaining during that summer, but she quickly developed warm friendships with both the members of the University community and the summer visitors.

At the July 1870 meeting of the trustees of the University, a recommendation was adopted providing that the necessary steps be taken to develop the University according to its original plan. Some board members felt that the financial instability of the existing institution made such action premature, but they were overruled, and schools of ancient languages, modern languages, mathematics, metaphysics (which included English literature, rhetoric, and composition), civil engineering, chemistry, and moral science were established. The University of the South now became a university in the full sense. The preparatory school continued under the same administration.[2] Willie became one of the first students in the University and pleased his parents greatly by winning the Alabama medal for academic excellence.

The Gorgases decided that their prospects were secure enough to go ahead with the construction of their home, which was completed by May 1871. The dormitory was now left free to house student boarders. The new house had ample room for visitors, and the Gorgases were seldom without them. Some of the trustees usually stayed with them during the annual board meeting, and there were other University guests to be entertained. Mary Aiken and her two children came in mid-July 1871 for an extended stay; and before they left, Mary made plans to come back to Sewanee as a dormitory matron. Clara Gayle, who had moved to Sewanee with the Gorgases, made her home in Alabama after the marriage of her daughter, Helen, to James Locke of Greensboro in December 1871; but she frequently visited at Sewanee, as did the Bayne family.

In September Jessie and Mamie, now fifteen and nearly fourteen, were sent to Columbia, Tennessee, to the boarding school their mother had attended. Amelia wanted her daughters to have this experience and felt that with the money she earned by having student boarders she could afford to give it to them.

The additional expenses incurred by the change to university status did increase the financial difficulties of the University, and in January 1872 Josiah took advantage of the winter holiday to go to New Orleans and Mobile to try to sell subscriptions for "University Bonds," which the Board of Trustees had authorized as a means of raising the badly needed funds.[3] While the continuing economic depression in the South made Josiah's mission only partially successful, it brought him and, vicariously, his wife great personal pleasure. His traveling companion was their twelve-year-old daughter, Minnie, still the belle of the family. She was reported to have been "heart-broken" the summer before when her friend General Shoup had married. She said he had promised to wait for her to grow up.

Josiah and Minnie stayed with the Baynes in New Orleans, and Josiah enjoyed seeing many old friends again, among them Judge Campbell, who was now practicing law there. The Baynes invited several of the Confederate Ordnance staff members for dinner with their former chief. Josiah wrote Amelia, "I wish all these civilities could be bestowed on you. You would enjoy them so much more than I do. Tho' I trust I am not ungrateful for them." He also observed, "Wife, darling, Maria does not live as comfortably as we do. I suppose it is the want of good servants. I doubt whether there is anywhere a home more thoroughly enjoyable than ours—thanks to its presiding divinity."[4]

By mid-February Josiah was back at Sewanee making preparations for the opening of the next school term. Early in March Amelia had her teeth removed. This event caused some anticipatory dread in the family. Although the thought probably remained unexpressed, the death of her mother following a tooth extraction must have been uppermost in their minds. However, all went well, and two weeks later she was sufficiently recovered to write Jessie:

Don't think that I forgot your birthday & that on the 17th you will be 16 years old almost a grown[-]up-lady—I am impatient you know for the time to come when you & Mamie will be my sweet companions & grown[-]up-daughters never to leave me until a dearer than even a Mother claims you—

I think my child that I have nothing more to ask of the good Father than that he will continue his loving care of you & preserve in your heart the grace he has vouchsafed to bestow upon you—Your influence & example has been very great upon your brothers & sisters & your mission will be high & holy if you influence to good those immediately around you—

The boys are coming in rapidly & the opening services today were quite imposing—... Willie arrived on Wed. looking so well & happy—I send a photograph which is not however a good one making him appear too sober—Ma & Eddie are at Cowan & will be up in an hour.[5] ... Ria & Richie have gone to the depot to meet Grand-Ma & are in a state of great delight—Gen. Shoup sat an hour with us last night & sent his especial love & kisses to you.

Dear Nana sends you each a gold piece for birth-day & it is the nest egg for your future fortunes if you do not give it into my keeping.

I am afraid she will not get off for Easter though I will try & persuade her to go to Nashville if not further to Baltimore—she will be so much happier after she sees a Priest—... I have not finished your dresses—but know you will excuse me as my house has been so full of company & I too have been right sick—I am perfectly well again—Father talks a great deal of his absent daughters & sends many kisses—All will rejoice to see you home again. ...[6]

In June the girls wrote their mother about plans for the end of the school term and received the following answer:

> I cannot understand from your notes whether or not you really desire to remain to the examination & concert.
>
> I will make no serious objections if you prefer to remain but I am utterly opposed to public exhibitions for girls—I presume they are necessary to satisfy a large portion of the patrons of the school but many of its best friends would be glad to see them abolished.
>
> Write me by return mail what you desire to do without fear of offending your teachers—they are too wise to desire to prevent entire confidence between Mother & children—Send me the measure of your waist & the length of your skirt—I must send to Louisville for the swiss muslin—I will get some ideas of a pretty dress from Mrs. Munford who dresses beautifully & is very sweet & obliging—I have a beautiful pink rose which I can lend Mamie & I suppose your pink sashes will just suit.
>
> We fully expect Aunt Ria about the 12th she will only remain a few days—just long enough to establish the children comfortably—
>
> Aunt Mary will come as soon as she can get possession of Tremlette or a part of it which will be the last of this month or the 1st of July—... Nana & Ria are in a great state of excitement about their trip to Nashville—They want to go the last of the week but I fear Nana will scarcely be strong enough. She is up but looks pale & feeble.—Father has been a little indisposed for two or three days but nothing serious—Minnie appears very happy to get back home & is the most useful little creature to me—She is not sociable with her young friends not having paid a single visit since her return—I enclosed a note from Aunt Eliza who sounds very feeble—how much I wish you & your Father could make her a little visit this summer— ... Be sure to write without delay & be decided as to whether you want to remain to the concert—All send love[7]

When the Board of Trustees held its annual meeting in July 1872, Bishop Quintard submitted his resignation as vice-chancellor of the University and asked that a resident head be appointed to replace him. General Gorgas was unanimously elected to serve a three-year term. In accepting the office Gorgas included a word of caution in his message to the trustees:

I am not fully informed of the action taken by the board on the matter of finance but unless income and expenditures have been so proportioned as to insure the success of the former, all the efforts of a vice-chancellor cannot avert embarrassment and inefficiency. I can only hope that the board has fully considered resources and appreciated our expenditures; and that they have not left this vital point in doubt. Expenditures estimated for are always certain to occur, resources confidently relied on are seldom fully attained. The experience of the past year warns us against an overestimate of our receipts.[8]

Unfortunately, these admonitions were little heeded. Still worried, in October Josiah noted, "We have our financial troubles and rub along with difficulty. Bishop Quintard goes out now on a tour of collection, hoping to get a large endowment for the University."[9]

During the summer Amelia had welcomed her sister, Mary Aiken, who came as matron of Tremlett Hall, bringing her children Gayle and Carrie and her sister-in-law, Miss Carrie Aiken. Mary was grateful for the opportunity to support herself and her family, and she was soon at home in the community, which included many friends from South Carolina. The most important of these in the life of the University was the Reverend William Porcher DuBose, who had become the chaplain at Sewanee in 1871.[10]

On January 30, 1873, Amelia finally set out on a long-discussed visit to New Orleans and Mobile, which she had not seen since she left for Maine in 1856. Her warm reception in both cities delighted her. From Mobile she wrote her husband with some amusement that one friend declared that she should not conceal her "beautiful" snow-white hair with caps, and that she would therefore abandon them except for morning wear.[11] Another letter declared:

I am such a belle among my old friends that I have only the hour just after breakfast in which to write.

My appearance at Church on Sunday announced my arrival to my friends & yesterday I had a regular reception—Such a number of visitors arrived in quick succession that a neighbor came over to see what the matter was—this is all very gratifying to me—Mrs. Schroeder thinks I could be elected on the congressional ticket as my popularity is as great among the colored aristocracy as the white folks. . . .

Even in her new role as social butterfly Amelia retained her strong interest in the practical. Sewanee affairs seemed uppermost in her mind:

> I don't know what we are to do about receiving boys into our family; many more would come from Mobile if I could take them— Judge Bragg is under the impression that his sons are to come to us when school opens—Of course I must take little Beverly Brown since he has no Mother—Mrs. Goldthwaite gives me a very handsome lunch at half past 2 today—all the fashionable are invited to meet me & of course I will wear my very best & stick out in the most approved style. . . .
>
> Poor Dr. Nott is sinking rapidly & sees no one but his physicians— . . . Mrs. Hammond has three boys for us & I am to see her tonight & talk the matter over with her. If I had more time I think I could bring a good many boys back with me— . . .
>
> I would be glad if Hans could arrange Hollys room before school opens & the upper part of the Dormitory—The door requires something to prevent the rain beating under & Mr. Eaton's room ought to have the paper in the corner renewed & a little paint would improve appearances wonderfully—I feel exactly as if the school were entirely yours. I am so anxious that everything should appear well to the visitors who tell me they intend spending a portion of next summer on the Mt.—

She concluded, "Dear Little Minnie is very faithful in writing me—& my children are all sweet & good & my husband the dearest & best that ever blessed a happy wife."

During her stay in Mobile she found time to visit her father's grave in Magnolia Cemetery, where she found everything looking "sweet" and well kept, and to see her brother Matt who was being cared for at Mt. Vernon.

She arrived in New Orleans in time for the Mardi Gras festivities. She wrote her family that the Mystic Krewe procession was "really magnificent" and that the ball reminded her of pictures she had seen of some royal pageant. "Mr. Bayne and Maria are so kind & make every moment of my stay charming," she added.[12]

Amelia returned to a life at Sewanee that was increasingly

wrapped up in the lives of her own children and of the school boys in her charge. Jessie and Mamie were enrolled in a new school that opened in 1873 at Monteagle, just a few miles from Sewanee. It was conducted by two ladies from Mississippi, who were encouraged and assisted in the undertaking by the Reverend Mr. DuBose. Willie was an active participant in university activities, acting as captain of the first nine of the Hardee baseball club and president of the football club. The ladies of the community made the baseball uniforms and provided an enthusiastic rooting section at the games.[13]

Amelia's constant interest in the welfare of the students won her the reputation of being "the boys' best friend." On one occasion several boys were having a card game in their room when they heard a knock on the door. Calling "Come in," they hastily shoved the cards into their laps under the table. Their visitor was Mrs. Gorgas, who looked around and quietly remarked, "That is the most suspicious looking table and the most innocent looking set of boys I ever saw. I have just come to tell you that the General is on an Inspection tour, and you had better look out."[14]

The summer of 1874 followed what had become a familiar pattern for the Gorgas family. The Baynes were with them much of the season, and the Gorgases enjoyed providing entertainment for the younger members of the family. Willie selected a pony for young Charlie Bayne's pleasure, while Amelia gave a fancy-dress party to celebrate his sister Minna's sixth birthday in July. There were many visitors on the mountain, and the recently enlarged chapel was frequently filled for the two services held each day. Funds for the chapel addition were augmented by a popular form of entertainment, the penny reading. Amelia was hostess for several of these events, which consisted of instrumental music and singing as well as readings and simple refreshments.[15]

General Edmund Kirby Smith joined the faculty as professor of mathematics in 1875 to succeed General Shoup, who had left Sewanee to go into parish work. General Smith had grown up in St. Augustine, Florida, and his connections with many members of the Sewanee community were of long standing. Amelia remembered her pleasant visit with the general and his wife in Baltimore in 1866. The Kirby Smiths' home at Sewanee was called Powhatan Hall. Their large family of children and their dogs, Ned and Dick, soon became a familiar part of the Sewanee scene. Amelia became the godmother of one of the children.

Though enrollment at the University continued to climb, financial pressures continued to mount, and Josiah was increasingly concerned that the board was unwilling to take strong action. To add to his worries, his health began to give way early in the winter of 1875. He suffered such severe pain in his right arm that he was unable to rest at night without medicine, and he often got up several times to warm his arm by the fire. Amelia was alarmed about his condition and encouraged him to go to New Orleans during the vacation to consult doctors there and to see if a change in climate would bring him any relief.

Following her advice, Josiah joined Willie in Louisiana for several weeks. (The young man had completed his studies at Sewanee in December and was working in his uncle Thomas Bayne's law office and preparing for entrance examinations for West Point.) Josiah was told by the doctors he consulted that he was suffering from atrophy or wasting of the arm muscle and that his pain might cease with the disappearance of the substance of the muscle. Not greatly encouraged by their diagnosis, he returned to Sewanee for the new term, still suffering. He tried the baths at North Carolina Warm Springs in June but received little relief. Nevertheless, he continued to carry out his duties so efficiently that at their August 1875 meeting the trustees elected him to a new five-year term as vice-chancellor.[16]

Much of Amelia and Josiah's attention at this time was focused on Willie's future. He received his bachelor's degree at the commencement exercises on August 5 and celebrated his twenty-first birthday two months later with a dinner party for some of his friends. He was "ardently prosecuting the pursuit of a cadetship at West Point" against the wishes of his parents, who did not want him to have to endure the rootless existence of the professional soldier. In deference to their views he tried the law for almost a year, but when he decided that it was not the career he wanted, they accepted his decision. Josiah wrote, "I am doing all I can to help him, tho' it grieves me to see him so infatuated about West Point and so opposed to the law, in which he would have so capital an opportunity with his uncle

Bayne."[17] Both Amelia and Josiah wrote letters to influential friends in his behalf and provided their son with money to live in the district where they thought his chances were best, but their efforts were to no avail. Appointments were in great demand, and when Willie reached the age of twenty-two in the fall of 1876, he was no longer eligible. Still certain that he wanted a military career, he decided that his best course would be to go to New York to study medicine in preparation for service as an army surgeon. Ironically, the profession that seemed initially second best to him turned out to be the one that brought forth all his talents, and he was soon sending home enthusiastic accounts of his studies.

Josiah's failing health and the University's financial situation continued to be dual burdens for him during 1876. He attempted to alleviate both problems on another trip to New Orleans in January and February. Amelia had earlier written Willie that though his father was not losing weight, he was growing more nervous and that she felt he needed change and rest. It must have pleased her to hear that Josiah was seeing many old friends and talking to Jefferson Davis about material on the Confederate Ordnance Bureau for a book Davis was writing. He was also successful in collecting some funds for the University, chiefly through special church offerings. As solicitous of his family's well being as Amelia had been when she was away, he wrote her, "As soon as you get a cold snap let Hans kill a hog and make him look out and buy a sow either with young ones or about to have a litter. Please remember this important matter."[18]

Josiah returned home by way of Mobile, where he visited Sarah Crawford, who was now taking boarders to stretch her slender resources, and consulted Amelia's cousin, Dr. Fountain Heustis, [19] about his condition. He returned to Sewanee feeling "pretty well" and impatient to get back to his work, but by fall his condition had worsened. He began to be troubled by a numbness in his left leg and arm and feared the onset of paralysis. Amelia showed her anxiety over his condition in her frequent letters to Willie, who was applying himself diligently to his studies at Bellevue Hospital. While she often asked for his counsel about his father's health, she gave him a good deal of motherly advice in return. She worried about Willie's health, his finances, and the state of his wardrobe, urging him to buy a new coat if his old one looked shabby. "Do get a nice one & just remember that half a physician's success depends upon his appearance."[20]

Remembering how helpful friends had been to her and her family at critical periods in their lives, she encouraged Willie to try to meet some of her old friends and his father's relatives who lived in the city. Dr. William Polk, who had worked with Josiah at Brierfield, and his wife Ida were invariably kind and helpful, and Mrs. Isaac Bell, who had renewed her correspondence with Amelia after the difficult years of the war, also welcomed him. Soon after Willie's arrival in New York he received an invitation to "Sister" Bell's wedding. His mother instructed him: "You will of course be present at the ceremony in the church & if guests are not required to be in full evening dress, at the two o'clock reception at the house—If your duties prevent you from going be sure to call & explain why you did not attend—these affairs demand so much ceremony." Willie wrote his mother about meeting "Ikey" Bell, who had been the guest of honor at the almost disastrous birthday party so many years before. She replied, "So Ikey is a fat middle aged man—it sounds strangely to me for I have not seen him since he was a slender lad of 13 or 14 years." Josiah's nephew, William E. Dorsheimer, son of his sister Sarah, was serving as lieutenant-governor of New York and after meeting Willie wrote a cordial letter to Josiah and Amelia.[21]

Writing letters served as an outlet for Amelia's love for her oldest child, but she missed him greatly, writing at Christmastime 1876, "If you were only with us our circle would be complete—I do not indulge in useless repinings for I know my darling is pursuing the career which will make him a good useful & great man—We feel so relieved that you are satisfied that the move to N. Y. was a good one—sympathy with one's duties ensures success in half the undertakings of this world."

Josiah again made a winter trip to New Orleans in 1877, this time taking Mamie, whom he left for an extended visit with the Baynes. They gave her a taste of New Orleans social life including visits to the theater, balls, and Mardi Gras festivities.

Soon after his return to Sewanee Josiah wrote Willie that his mother was concerned at not hearing from him for nearly two weeks: "You had better make a habit of writing to someone at home *every week*. It will save your mother much anxiety."[22] Willie's letters began to come more regularly, and he apparently needed no further admonition.

There seemed no end to and no solution for the problem of monetary support for the University of the South. No regular income came from the Episcopal Church, and the fund-raising methods used were not able to arouse the needed response. Even the income from student fees was seldom up to expectations, as many students paid only partial tuition. Undoubtedly there were other administrative problems as well, but Josiah was nevertheless stunned when the Board of Trustees at their meeting in July 1877 adopted a resolution stating, "That in the opinion of this board its acting and responsible head and the officer of its discipline, the vice-chancellor, should be, if practicable, a clerk in Holy Orders . . .; and that to this end the vice-chancellor be informed of this preamble and these resolutions in order that he may have full time to make provision for himself, and in such a way as shall least affect the University by any sudden change and all, if possible, within the next twelve months ensuing."[23] How much General Gorgas's health had to do with bringing about this action and how much basic disagreement there was about the best way to administer a church school, it is hard to judge. When things are not going well, a scapegoat is often sought, and in this case it was the vice-chancellor. Josiah had staunch supporters among the board members, however, and the action of the trustees was not without opposition.

To Amelia the treatment of her husband was almost unforgiveable. Her immediate reaction was one of righteous indignation, and her bitterness had abated very little when she wrote Willie in October, "We are anxious the boys shall understand when they go away that your Father will not be at the head of the school next year. I am sure it will affect the prosperity of the school & I sincerely hope it will. . . . I am not willing for your Father to work any longer for the school—or in any way to be responsible for it. They treated him with the greatest ingratitude & I hope they will reap their reward." Two months later she wrote her son, "I shall be a happy woman as soon as your Father can turn his back upon Sewanee and we all forget the existence of such a place."

With the security he so strongly desired to give his family once again shattered, Josiah wasted no time in making inquiries about teaching positions open in other universities. He even considered starting a military school on Lookout Mountain, but being without capital, he realized this project would not be practical for him.

In the midst of her anxieties, Amelia was happy to see one member of the family enjoy the winter. Eighteen-year-old Minnie represented her family at the wedding of Mamie Bayne in November and stayed on in New Orleans for the winter season. Amelia had been dubious about the plan at first, writing Willie, "Minnie is very anxious to accept her Aunt Ria's invitation to spend the winter in New Orleans—if possible I would gladly give her the pleasure—But a season in N. O. entails expenses we had better not afford just now—however I will not throw impediments in the way."[24] The Baynes' wishes prevailed in the end, and Minnie enjoyed the season to the utmost. She was a guest at a party described by her aunt as the handsomest one she had ever attended. Minnie wrote Jessie: "The way I did dance and how I did enjoy myself! As I was a stranger I expected to be a perfect wall-flower but I danced all the time and had three escorts to supper, which Aunt Ria tells me is a compliment few ladies receive." She paid calls with her aunt and wrote her family of going to see Jefferson Davis's niece and Judge Campbell's family. "Mrs. Lay [Judge Campbell's daughter] was very affectionate—said that she felt she had a claim on me as she nursed me in Richmond when we all had scarlet fever. I feel like thanking Mother every time I go anywhere. I am always meeting friends of hers who are so kind to me on her account."

She sent word to Mamie that a gentleman friend of Mamie's had come to see her and given her several hints about how to behave at parties: "Among other things he said not to pretend to be so fond of dancing as to jump up from the supper table after sitting for a few moments, for gentlemen always like supper. I think this has helped me along more than anything else." One of Minnie's callers was Mrs. William Taylor Palfrey, whose son George had boarded with the Gorgases at Sewanee and was a special friend of Minnie's. "Mrs. Palfrey is one of the sweetest ladies I have ever met. . . . She would make a charming mother-in-law!! . . . I have tried my very best to be homesick but I can't succeed; Still no one could leave such a home as mine without missing it, and I suppose I would be wretched in any other place than N. O."[25]

While Minnie was enjoying her social life, her father was continuing his search for a new position. He spent the month of February in Washington looking into possible openings there, but it was soon evident to him that the capital city was not the answer. "I don't think my love," he wrote Amelia, "I shall ever want a position here. I am not in love with the place or its atmosphere. I believe I had rather teach than hold a place here at the will of the politicians." On a visit to General Stephen V. Benét at the United States Army Ordnance Office, he was taken to see the weather instruments at the Signal Office and was promised a small set for Sewanee. With his customary generosity of spirit, he wrote his wife, "Let us do what we can for it for Auld Lang Syne." Later in his visit he commented in a letter to her, "The philosophical spirit of your last letter cheers me. I think we can turn the whole matter to our advantage in the end."[26] Evidently time was helping her to accept the blow that had come to them.

By April the pain in Josiah's arm had returned with some violence, and their future plans were still uncertain. Amelia wrote Willie that she longed for his father to have a rest from responsibility. She endeavored to keep their home life as normal as possible in the face of many uncertainties, and their daughters cooperated with her efforts. She told Willie that Jessie had a fine garden and kept busy with her little school and that Mamie was developing into a good seamstress and housekeeper and was of great assistance to her. Ria was doing well at boarding school, and Minnie was still in New Orleans. Richie, now fourteen, lived at home and attended the Sewanee grammar school. He took great pleasure in his half-setter, half-Newfoundland puppy, which his mother said was almost as much trouble as a baby—"but we willingly endure the annoyance for the pleasure it gives the boy."[27]

Happily the Gorgases' uncertainty was not to last much longer. On July 8 Josiah sent Willie a brief note:

Lest the girls might forget to write you, I merely write a line to say that I have been elected President of the University at Tuscaloosa and have accepted the position. We are all delighted at this piece of good fortune, due entirely to the friendship of Col. Dawson whom you will remember.[28] I shall go there at the close of this month, and stay there a week and shall then return and remain until the middle of September. The family will probably not go until December. The children will tell you more about it.[29]

HOME
TO ALABAMA

GENERAL GORGAS LEFT for Tuscaloosa on July 30, 1878, after notifying Bishop William Green, chancellor of the University of the South, that engagements elsewhere would prevent him from attending the board meeting and that he had appointed the senior professor, Dr. Elliott, as his substitute "until such time as the wishes of the Board may be made known." Whatever his private thoughts about his treatment by the board may have been, he showed only his innate courtesy in his farewell message, which concluded, "Allow me, Reverend Sir, in severing our official relations, to express to you the reverent and affectionate regard I entertain for you personally. With the earnest wish that your useful and noble life may be prolonged, / I remain your obedient servant / J. Gorgas."[1]

Amelia and her family remained at Sewanee for several more months, but her satisfaction with their prospects for the future is clearly reflected in a letter Mary Aiken wrote to her sister-in-law (Eliza A. Woodward) shortly before Josiah's departure:

> The mountain is crowded with visitors & will be very lively by next week. Gen. G. expects to hand in his resignation the first day of the meeting of the Board & will leave for Tuscaloosa the next morning to be absent about two weeks. They will have a comfortable and beautiful home there & I think everything has been ordered for the best. The position is so much better in every respect than this & even if that had not been offered, the Professorship at Baton Rouge would have been as good in point of salary. A great many letters of congratulations have been received & all speak of their going home. We have so

many friends in Alabama, I think it will be best for our children to
live where we are best known.[2]

Amelia's pleasure over her husband's new position was naturally
somewhat clouded by her concern for his health, which remained an
almost constant worry. He returned to Sewanee from Tuscaloosa in
mid-August suffering considerable pain and decided to seek relief at
Blount Springs, a popular Alabama resort, for a few days before
assuming the University presidency in September. As he turned
toward his new responsibilities, he wrote Amelia that he had given
up all hope of ever being well, but that he prayed fervently that he
would remain able to do his duty to his family. "If it is no worse than
just now I shall bear it without further repining and I think I can
sustain all the duties and labors of my position."[3]

As he had done so often before, Josiah prepared his wife for her
prospective home through his letters. Establishing himself temporarily in a downtown hotel, he renewed his acquaintance with old
friends and was introduced to his new faculty. They were at this
time a rather small group, for the student body numbered only
about eighty. William S. Wyman taught Latin language and literature; John C. Calhoun, a great-nephew of the South Carolina
senator, Greek; B. F. Meek, English; and William A. Parker,
modern languages. Eugene A. Smith, who was the state geologist,
and Joshua Foster instructed students in the sciences; and Hender-
son M. Somerville and John M. Martin, in law. William J. Vaughn
was professor of mathematics. Thomas C. McCorvey held the post
of commandant of cadets and acting professor of mental and moral
philosophy and political economy. Professor Wyman also acted as
librarian for the University.[4]

The members of the faculty welcomed their new president cor-
dially. Josiah wrote his wife that Professor Meek, a bachelor who
lived at the hotel where he was staying, was "very pleasant and
companionable," and he told her that he had been invited to dine
with Professor Wyman and had seen Professor Parker's triplets, "a
pretty group." He also met Dr. Peter Bryce, the head of the State
Asylum for the Insane, and his wife, a "most attractive and cultivated
woman." He wrote Amelia that he thought the Bryces would be

their "pleasant neighbors." (The Asylum property adjoined that of the University.)

In October Josiah moved into the handsome President's Mansion on the campus. Built in 1841 the white stuccoed brick mansion had a double curved stairway leading to the elevated entrance and six Ionic columns supporting the roof of the entrance portico. He sent Amelia sketches and measurements of the rooms, and their letters were full of plans for the furnishing of the house. Willie paid an autumn visit to Sewanee and arrived in Tuscaloosa in November accompanied by his brother Richie, Richie's beloved dog, and a trunkful of household goods to tide Josiah over until Amelia's arrival. Willie had to return to New York after a short stay, but Richie remained with his father and attended Mr. Verner's school. Josiah reported to Amelia that Richie's large dog was an unfailing source of pleasure and that Richie's appetite was also "unfailing," "25 oysters and two or three sweet potatoes seem to sit lightly on his young stomach."[5]

Amelia was not lonely during her last months at Sewanee. Sarah, Millie, and Sallie Crawford were with her during much of the fall,[6] and she spent many hours at Tremlett Hall helping Mary Aiken nurse her dying sister-in-law. Mary planned to move into the Gorgas residence when Amelia left. Josiah was not in a hurry to sell the house, feeling it important that his family should still own a home if he should become incapacitated.[7]

By early December Amelia and Josiah were writing about final arrangements for the move. It was a large undertaking for Amelia to manage alone, and there were many other calls upon her time. She and Mary were at Carrie Aiken's bedside when she died on December 16, and Amelia read the prayers for the dying from the Book of Common Prayer. Two days later she was the only guest not a member of one of the two families at the wedding of the widowed William Porcher DuBose to Mrs. Yerger, who had taught the Gorgas girls at Monteagle.

The tributes paid her before her departure from Sewanee helped ease the bitterness Amelia had felt at Josiah's dismissal. She was much moved by a note from Bishop Green:

Nothing but my feeble heart has prevented me from saying "Good

bye" to you, and accompanying it with my best wishes and my
fatherly blessing. You will carry with you the affectionate remem-
brance of all our Mountain and I know that your old friends, and native
state will be only too glad to have you once more with them. Please
bid the Girls "Good bye" for me; and assure my good friend, the
General that Sewanee contains no warmer admirer of himself and
family than, Yours most truly . . . [8]

Amelia left many devoted friends at Sewanee and a reputation for
gracious hospitality. She and the girls and Anne Kavanaugh left for
Tuscaloosa a few days after Christmas, spending a night at the Read
House in Chattanooga before proceeding on their way. They arrived
in Tuscaloosa at ten o'clock at night in the pouring rain but received
a warm welcome from Josiah and Richard. The freight car bearing
their furniture had preceded them, and Josiah had unpacked and
placed things "temporarily," certain that his wife would "desire
changes." He greeted his daughters, who were now all grown, ranging in age from seventeen to twenty-two, with invitations to attend a
New Year's Eve Ball and to assist at Mrs. Bryce's New Year's reception.

In a letter to Willie, Amelia described her delight in her new
surroundings:

> I believe I have not written you from our charming new home
> where we are all as happy as the day is long. It is impossible to
> imagine a man more improved than your dear Father—he is once
> more bright & cheerful & hopeful—working with all his old time
> energy & interest—A call meeting of the trustees is in session here
> now & it is charming to see with what confidence & respect they treat
> your Father—the faculty too are in perfect accord & life is altogether
> different here from what it was at Sewanee. We have been hand-
> somely entertained by every member of the faculty & by Dr. and
> Mrs. Bryce & in our turn—we gave a nice lunch to the trustees & the
> faculty on Monday—Everyone calls to see us—making us most wel-
> come. [9]

Colonel McCorvey wrote his fiancée that the Gorgases' luncheon
"was a very enjoyable occasion. Mrs. Gorgas plays the hostess to
perfection." [10]

Amelia's enjoyment of her new life was short-lived. Early in February she was called back to Sewanee by the illness of Mary Aiken. She hoped to move her sister to Tuscaloosa but found her too ill to travel and had to stay in Tennessee to nurse her. Josiah wrote, "All is going on as well as we can expect without you! But we all miss you sadly." A few days later he sent another letter saying that they were eagerly awaiting her arrival with Mary, "saved by your devotion."[11] However, Amelia was still at Sewanee on February 23 when Josiah suffered a stroke. His dread forebodings had been realized, and though he was not paralyzed, his speech was affected and there was grave concern over his condition. Amelia returned home immediately to care for him. She sent Willie almost daily reports of his father's condition and relied on his medical knowledge for support. On March 8 she reported hopefully:

> Dr. Searcy has just left & says he is entirely satisfied with his improvement which though slow is still a little each day.[12] The poor patient however is very much discouraged & said this morning that he had no sense at all. . . . Professor Wyman takes your Father's place & everything seems to go on smoothly & well. . . . The Drs think he will be able to do some duty in a month & all seem more than willing to do his work until he recovers. But I can see that your dear Father dreads the possibility of never recovering his impaired faculties. . . . My courage & hope has not flagged for a moment & I keep his room as bright & cheerful as possible—hiding from him everything that could worry him. . . .

As soon as Thomas Bayne heard of Josiah's illness he wrote Amelia, "I am appalled at the news of your dear good husband. I received a most cheerful letter from him dated on the 22nd. He was so anxious for the success of the University—Always works so hard for anything he has in hand—is so unselfish. . . . You know I scarcely give place even to you in my love for him." Maria Bayne was also seriously ill, and her husband did not tell her at once of Josiah's illness. Bayne sent Amelia $250 to help meet any extra demands she might have, adding that he knew she had incurred extra expense in attending "Sister Mary." "You have been called upon to make great sacrifices this winter. It looks to me as if all our misfortunes come upon us at once."[13]

By the middle of March Mary Aiken was well enough to join the Gorgas household in Tuscaloosa. She wrote Maria of the "blessed repose & quiet of this charming place" and urged her to join them for her own restoration to health. She said that she found General Gorgas better than she had expected and that she thought he would recover, though the process would be slow. She commented on Amelia's devotion, tact, and resourcefulness, stating that she was beginning to think her more than mortal.[14]

In April Amelia and Josiah were able to go to Mobile for a visit with Sarah and consultation with Dr. Heustis, who told Josiah that he must be patient and not trouble himself about the future. Amelia reported to Willie that though his father was discouraged, he was bright and cheerful generally and that she hoped he had made up his mind to submit to what he could not avert. She added that he had decided that he should submit his resignation to the Board of Trustees in July. They would accept the inevitable if the trustees felt they must choose a successor before Josiah could hope to resume his duties. Added to their own worries was their distress over the news from New Orleans that Maria was no better and that her daughter Mamie's young husband, George Behn, was dying of tuberculosis. Maria was taken to Chicago for treatment and died there on July 11, 1879, at the age of forty-five.

The University of Alabama trustees granted Josiah a leave of absence at their July meeting, but by September Josiah and Amelia had come to the conclusion that he could not in fairness to the University continue to hold the presidency. His resignation was accepted, but the Board appointed him librarian at a salary of $400 a year and made Amelia hospital matron, for which she would be paid three dollars a day for each boy placed in her charge. In addition, the Pratt House, which had served as the dining hall in the early days of the school, was provided as a residence for them free of charge. Amelia wrote Willie that the Trustees had behaved handsomely to them: "The position of Librarian was created for him at the suggestion of the faculty, who greatly desire to retain him at the Univ. I think he will enjoy the light duty. Minnie & Mamie will be his assistants & perform all the drudgery of the office."

In the midst of their troubles, Amelia and Josiah found great comfort in the progress of their elder son. William Crawford Gorgas had received his M.D. degree in June 1879 and begun his internship at Bellevue Hospital in New York City. He kept in close touch with his family and looked forward to the day when he could help with their expenses, especially those for Richard's education. He knew what a struggle it would be for them to provide even as much help as they had given him. Amelia wrote in October, "Our short twelve months have made such changes & brought about such sorrows that I do not ask to see the future."[15] She felt that their needs for the next year were provided for and that that was enough for the present.

The Gorgases now turned their attention to their new responsibility. The University library, originally housed in the Rotunda, had been totally destroyed by Croxton's Raiders in April 1865. Soon after the war, efforts were made by President Landon Cabell Garland, Professor Wyman, and other University officials to assemble the beginnings of a new collection. Novelist Augusta Evans Wilson was one of a number of Mobile citizens who made contributions from their private libraries. Professor and Mrs. Samuel Stafford of Tuscaloosa presented 245 volumes. After the reorganization of the University in 1871 valuable donations further enriched library holdings. Dr. F. A. P. Barnard, an early faculty member, presented an elegantly bound set of his new edition of *Johnson's Encylopedia*. By the time General Gorgas assumed the librarianship, the library contained over seven thousand volumes, housed in a room in the barracks.

Colonel McCorvey, who served as correspondent for a number of newspapers, described the library in an article printed in the *Montgomery Advertiser and Mail* on December 28, 1879:

> The books have been admirably classified and arranged by the Librarian, General Josiah Gorgas, late President of the University, who carries into everything he undertakes the habits of precision which he acquired in his soldierly training. The library is open to students under certain regulations, from 10 a.m. to 3 p.m. of each day except Sunday.[16]

The responsibility for the library passed gradually from Josiah to Amelia during the following year. She took over his duties temporarily early in 1880 when he and Richard went to New Orleans to visit

Tom Bayne and Mary Aiken, who was now helping her brother-in-law care for his motherless family. Amelia found the library work very much to her taste, and after Josiah had another stroke later in the year she took over his position in all but title.

Her older children were now able to provide support in a variety of ways. In June 1880 Willie received an appointment as surgeon in the U.S. Army, finally realizing his long-deferred dream of becoming an army officer. From his new post in Texas he sent monthly checks home to his always hard-pressed family. Jessie, though shy and retiring, was "the practical member of the family," and according to her mother, kept the family accounts with great accuracy and purchased their supplies in the most economical way possible. Minnie assisted her mother with the housekeeping and in the library, as Mamie had taken a teaching position in Talledega. Richard was a freshman at the University, and Maria was studying in Cincinnati.

In January 1881 Amelia wrote Thomas Bayne of receiving an unexpected return on some money she had invested in the Brierfield Iron Works and described for him her new daily routine:

> I spend from 11 o'clock to 2 in the Library leaving the domestic arrangements & household duties entirely to my willing daughters—As the library is a resort for the students & professors no one of them could sit here alone, & I find the duty very pleasant & the friendly intercourse with Professors & boys an advantage to me in my position as Hos. Matron. The health of the Uni is however marvellously good & I have had only one patient during this term—they are only sent to the Hos. in case of very serious illness.[17]

Many of the students were the sons of old friends and acquaintances, and they often stopped by the library for a few minutes' chat with her. She noted that she was often the only woman the young men ever saw on the campus.

The fall of 1881 brought to Amelia the pleasure of making plans for the marriage of her daughter Minnie to George Palfrey of St. Mary's Parish, Louisiana, the friend of Sewanee days, whose mother Minnie had envisaged as "a charming mother-in-law" on her New Orleans trip four years earlier. It was necessarily a quiet home ceremony and took place on December 29, the twenty-eighth anniver-

sary of Amelia and Josiah's wedding. Willie had been granted leave
for the occasion. Dressed in his uniform, he escorted the family's
beloved Nana, who was now very frail, into the parlor on his arm.
After the ceremony the young couple left immediately for their new
home in Louisiana.

Anne Kavanaugh's death came only a few weeks after Minnie's
wedding. Willie wrote from Texas, "It is a comfort to know that she
passed away so quietly. Indeed her whole sickness was accompanied
by very little pain—not as much as is usual in consumption. I hope I
may take death as calmly & look forward to it with as little fear as she
did."[18] Anne Kavanaugh had been with the Gorgases for nearly
twenty-five years. She was buried in the Evergreen Cemetery near
the University campus.

Josiah's health continued to worsen during the next year. He
occasionally showed improvement for short intervals, but it had
become plain to his family and friends that he could not recover.
Death came on May 15, 1883, at seven o'clock in the evening.
Amelia described his last hours in a letter to Sarah Crawford two
days later:

> It is all over & my darling lies near Ann, his faithful friend, covered
> with exquisite flowers—"crowns" & crosses—harps & pierced hearts
> are heaped upon his precious grave—Every honor that respect &
> affection & sympathy could suggest was paid to him & he so calm &
> unconscious of it all—Yes, I ought to have been prepared for I saw
> days ago that the end drew near, but you know wives cannot prepare
> for such a parting—I am listening for him & thinking how long I have
> been away from him & he wanting me so much—Even now, while I
> am writing in our room & I see his *vacant* bed I am ready at any
> moment to drop my pen & go to his assistance for he had grown very
> helpless.—
> I think it was on the 5th or 6th that he was overcome with a sudden
> weakness after being dressed & sitting in the front room—He looked
> almost dying & I sent for Dr. Searcy who found his pulse good &
> assured me that the stupor was only an increase of the brain trouble
> from which he might rally as he has so frequently done.—
> He did not again leave his bed except to relieve his restlessness by
> sitting for a moment in his large chair. On Sunday night at 9 o'clock I
> saw another change & sent over for Dr. Bryce who came immediately

& discovered a slight paralysis of the left arm—the Dr. returned at
9 o'clock on Monday morning & found him breathing stertorously & in
a few minutes a slight convulsion came on.

As soon as that passed the Dr. gave a hypodermic of morphine
which kept him perfectly quiet until 12 o'clock at night after which
the stertorous breathing returned—at day light I sent for Dr. Searcy
& when the good man looked at him I saw that my darling was
beyond his help—Dr. Bryce soon came over & the professors
gathered round their old chief never leaving him until his faint breath
expired with the last rays of the setting sun. At the last it was the
gentle breathing of an infant & not a sound disturbed the stillness of
the room as we knelt beside his bed, his dear hand in mine & my hot
cheek pressed to his cold forehead—Mrs. Bryce read for me in her
clear, sweet voice the parting prayer beginning "Go forth Christian
soul" etc.—

I wish all who loved him could have seen him; his fine face & noble
brow in the dignity of death was majestic & not a trace of suffering
was visible—

Dr. & Mrs. Bryce arranged everything & relieved us wholly from
care & anxiety as to the sad details—But my chief comfort was the
unexpected arrival of Mr. Bayne upon whom I seemed to be able to
cast a portion of my heavy burden—

He seemed gratified by the simple honors & universal sympathy of
these kind people & returned this morning feeling that he left us with
kind friends.—He would insist upon leaving $50.00 fearing we would
need it to meet the additional expenses—I hope we can return it to
him as soon as we hear from Willie who desires of course to assume all
charges—No brother could be kinder than Mr. Bayne & he was the
man my husband loved best in the world. (Not long ago I asked him if
he would like to see Mr. Bayne not knowing whether he would understand me—he replied "yes—oh yes—Bayne & I are very intimate—
we are brothers") I longed so for you to come that we determined to
telegraph for you, but then I remembered that you might not be able
to leave Mobile just at this time & countermanded the telegram. I
knew of course that Mary was obliged to stay with Edith. Lately two
or three times, as someone would come into the room he would ask if
that was Mary? but for 2 weeks he only spoke in whispers & could
only say yes & no. Sunday night as I lay on the bed beside him
thinking him unconscious—I asked him if he knew me & if he did I
implored him to press my hand which he did in the tenderest manner
& then turned his dear lips to mine for the last conscious kiss—(Mrs.

Thornton remained with me during the absence of the family & was very kind & sympathetic.)

But the sympathy is universal in [the] Community & I feel now as if I can never leave Tuscaloosa. I thought your lot quite filled or I could not have resisted the desire to lay him close to those he loved. But this is best for here his children can rest beside him when their time comes & as for me my poor body gives me not a thought—only I never want any extra expense bestowed upon it. I feel very restless & *dazed* & it has done me good to write. . . . I had a sweet letter from Mary yesterday. I will try & write her but I may lose my present strange strength & calmness. I cannot understand it—Love to my dear Millie & Sallie—My children comfort me with their love[19]

Letters of condolence poured in from near and far. Friends of Amelia's youth wrote from New York and Boston. Wartime associates of the Richmond days paid their tributes to Josiah. Jefferson Davis wrote from Beauvoir in Mississippi. From Sewanee Dr. DuBose wrote, "This is a fit opportunity to assure you of what I know you will believe—that among all those with whom I have been associated in the course of my life none have had a more certain & abiding place in my respect and affection than Gen. Gorgas and yourself—And I shall say also in my gratitude, for you were good & constant friends to me & Nannie from the moment I first came to this place."[20] General Shoup wrote from Texas, where he had met people who knew Willie and were full of praise for "Dr. Gorgas." From Mobile came a touching message from Mary Anne Gayle, who had been a slave in the Gayle family. Amelia had taught her to read and write and had sent her money from time to time through the years.

The Boards of Trustees of the University of the South and the University of Alabama both passed resolutions on the death of General Gorgas in recognition of his contributions to their institutions. Their tributes must have been both gratifying and comforting to Amelia. Burwell Boykin Lewis, Gorgas's successor as president of the University of Alabama, wrote her in July:

In addition to the appropriate resolutions adopted by the Board of Trustees at their recent meeting, commemorative of the distinguished services of your husband, Gen. Gorgas, I was directed by them to

refund to you all expenses of his funeral which at the suggestion of
your friends was put at $100.00. This was intended by them as an
evidence of their high appreciation of his character and services and as
a token of their sympathy with you and your children in your great
bereavement. Please sign the accompanying receipt. Permit me to
avail myself of this opportunity to again extend my individual sympathies with you and yours and express my sentiments of high regard
and friendship entertained for you all.[21]

Amelia's answer, of which she kept a copy, follows:

I return the receipt with a word of explanation—You cannot doubt
my appreciation of this generous & touching testimonial to my husband's memory, but I have the feeling that my son ought, as he has
done, to pay these sacred obligations.

My one object now is to erect a simple but appropriate shaft to his
memory & if the trustees would allow the donation to be so diverted I
would be so glad to make it the nucleus for a monumental fund. It
does not require stone or marble to perpetuate the memory of the
kindnesses received from the Trustees & from the faculty but it will
be a sweet satisfaction to me & to my children to know that they
materially assist in marking the last resting place of one they so honored in life & in death. I cannot tell you dear Mr. Lewis how much
your kindly words ameliorate the sadness of my life, & I have ever
known that I had the sympathy of your dear wife whose friendship I
so value.[22]

The "Minute on the Death of General Josiah Gorgas" adopted by
the Board of Trustees of the University of Alabama said in part:

Gen. Gorgas was no ordinary man. It is rare that we find a man in
whom all the virtues seem so happily blended; gentle and amiable as a
woman, yet on occasion he could be as stern and firm as a Roman.
Eminently conscientious in his own conduct, he had large charity for
others and was not ready to distrust or censure without abundant
cause. Of envy and its kindred passions he seemed to be without
knowledge. When he accepted a position, he gave to it all the powers
of his mind, all the energies of his body; he was diligent in business,
faithful to every trust, pure in life, scholarly in attainments, a model
husband and father, a genial companion, a devoted friend.

The world cannot but be the better for such men living in it, and has too few to spare, even one such, without feeling the loss.[23]

Amelia was especially pleased to learn that the obituary printed in the New Orleans *Times-Democrat* at the time of her husband's death was read in the Necrology of Graduates at the reunion of the graduates of the U.S. Military Academy. "I did not suppose they would notice his precious death but time I dare say has softened many of the asperities of the war."[24]

14

BELOVED LIBRARIAN

THE DEATH OF JOSIAH brought to a close a major chapter in Amelia's life, but there were many years yet to be lived, and Amelia faced them with courage. She pasted in her scrapbook a quotation that read, "The Past is a memory, the Future a hope, and the Present alone is ours." With this belief she could make each day meaningful.

Her adjustment to widowhood was made somewhat easier by the fact that she had already assumed many of the responsibilities of the head of the household during her husband's long illness. She had been the university librarian in fact if not in name for some time. Her children were, as always, a great comfort to her. The girls shared the household duties. Richard had not yet completed his education, and Amelia hoped to be able to give him the opportunity to prepare himself for whatever work would interest him most. Minnie provided her mother with a new interest, her first grandchild, who was born on March 24, 1883, and named Jessie Gorgas Palfrey for her grandfather and aunt.

Amelia spent the first summer after Josiah's death in going through his papers and in "cataloging" the library. In the latter task her niece Minna Bayne was her enthusiastic assistant. Amelia wrote her brother-in-law that she was surprised at his daughter's earnestness and perseverance and added that Minna seemed better pleased with the attentions of Professors Wyman and Parker, who joined them in the library each morning, than with those of her younger friends. "She seems very happy & contented in this quiet place taking her share of the household work & enjoying a simple game of croquet in the afternoon & a game of cards at night."[1]

Thomas Bayne had begun work on a sketch of the life of Josiah Gorgas for the *Southern Historical Papers*.[2] Amelia was delighted that it was he who was to carry out this assignment. "No one could write the biographical notice as well as you, who knew every thought of his honest and patriotic heart." She sent Bayne extracts from her husband's journal and other papers that she thought might prove helpful, including the "Notes on the Ordnance Department of the Confederate Government," which Josiah had written at the request of Jefferson Davis. She also recalled a story that she thought he might use: "Col. Baldwin, Gen. Lee's Ord officer, told me on his return to Richmond a few days after the surrender that Gen. Lee said to him at Appomattox Court House—'Tell Gorgas if other Depts had been conducted as was the Ord—I would not have been in such a strait as this' or words to that effect."

Working in the library kept Amelia abreast of the educational issues of the day. She wrote Tom Bayne that she wished he had time to read the discussions in the magazines for and against a classical education: "The scientific course has some very able advocates. Charles Francis Adams' paper at Harvard excites the ire of the Latin & Greek professors while the scientists applaud him. Our boys are constantly debating the subject in their societies & in assisting them to find articles I keep posted."[3] She wrote Willie that she did not think either of her surviving sisters was nearly as strong as she was, and she attributed her own strength "to my quiet country life & the pleasant occupation my position affords me. Such constant association with young people of necessity keeps me cheerful & hopeful." Another comment in a letter to her son provides an interesting insight into her thinking at this period in her life. Dr. Bryce, she wrote, "is still a devoted disciple of Herbert Spencer & so happy in his philosophy that he wants to convert all his friends. I listen to him always with interest but am too old to adopt new creeds which do not seem to me to contain the elements of principles of happiness as taught by the 'Master,' a greater far than Spencer."[4]

Amelia's contributions to the life of the University were publicly recognized by President Lewis in an address on May 5, 1884: "I wonder if the pen of Governor Gayle, pleading for the University was touched with the gift of prophecy that lifted the veil of futurity for him to see his own beloved and accomplished daughter at this day shedding the sweet sympathy of a Florence Nightingale in our hospital and the refining influence of a Lady Russell in our library."[5]

This was a period of great personal as well as professional satisfaction for Amelia. In the summer of 1882 Willie had met Marie Doughty of Cincinnati while she was visiting her sister and brother-in-law at Fort Brown, Texas. Just as years before yellow fever had brought Josiah and Amelia together, it played a significant part in the meeting of their son and his future wife. Dr. Gorgas's interest in the disease was so great that he had disobeyed orders of his superiors and gone into the yellow-fever section of the base hospital to examine patients there. Because he was not immune to the disease, he was immediately moved into the quarantined area, where he was soon called to treat Miss Doughty. She was so close to death that he was asked to read the burial service at her grave; but death was not to be her fate. She had begun to recover when Dr. Gorgas, too, fell victim to the disease. His case was not so serious as hers, and they were soon recuperating together.[6] He kept in touch with her when she returned to her home and wrote his family about her, but it was not until the summer of 1884 that he asked his mother to invite Marie to Tuscaloosa and arranged to secure leave to coincide with her visit.

Amelia wrote him, "I want you to marry the woman you love or loves you setting aside all preferences of the family. Your wife will be my daughter & I shall love her as such—if she permits me."[7] Marie and Amelia quickly established a warm relationship, and Marie later wrote in her biography of her husband:

> The picture Mrs. Gorgas made as she came from the dear old portico to greet me with the gracious manner so peculiarly her own made a lasting impression. She captured in one second the obdurate heart that had withstood for two years the siege of her handsome son. I then and there capitulated, and have always maintained that I fell in love with Mrs. Gorgas before I did with the Doctor, and that I owed my great happiness to her, for she aided in every way to bring about our engagement. That Mrs. Gorgas could so entirely forget self in her desire to further the happiness of her son in love with a young Northern girl who was almost an entire stranger to her, showed as perhaps nothing else the strength of her beautiful and unselfish character.[8]

The year 1885 brought great joy to Amelia with the birth of a grandson, William Taylor Palfrey, in Tuscaloosa on January 30 and the marriage of Willie and Marie in Cincinnati in September. The couple came to Tuscaloosa immediately after their wedding. Amelia gave an informal reception for them soon after their arrival, and a week later Mamie entertained them with a "progressive euchre party." Both events were reported in the society section of the New Orleans *Times-Democrat*. Willie and Marie returned to his post at Fort Randall, North Dakota, early in October.

In spite of the unaccustomed excitement at home, Amelia did not neglect her duties at the library. On October 2, 1885, the *Times-Democrat* reported:

> Mrs. Gen. Gorgas, the librarian of the University of Alabama, today informed THE TIMES-DEMOCRAT correspondent that the Hon. J. Walker Fearn, United States minister to Greece, had presented the library of that institution with a large and valuable collection of rare books. Many of these volumes were purchased and owned by the grandfather of the donor, Hon. John W. Walker, the first United States Senator from Alabama. It is a fitting destiny that they should come back to the chief educational institution of the State which so often honored him, although he did not live to see that institution established.[9]

Amelia continued to carry out her work efficiently and graciously through a number of changes in administration. President Lewis died in October 1885, and Professor Wyman served as acting president until the appointment of General Henry D. Clayton in June 1886. Clayton was especially interested in the physical facilities of the library, which had recently been moved to the main floor of Clark Hall, an imposing new building dedicated in June 1885. When the original plans for shelf arrangements in the new quarters proved inadequate, Clayton himself submitted new ones. Amelia's chair in the new library was one that had been built to accommodate the gigantic Dixon Lewis when he served in the state legislature; it had come to the University with other furnishings when the state capital was moved to Montgomery. Little Jessie Palfrey sometimes sat under the chair as she cut paper dolls, almost hidden by her grandmother's skirts.

In March 1886 a post office for the University was authorized, and the job of postmistress was added to Amelia's other duties. The new post office was set up in the back hall on the ground floor of the

Gorgases' campus home. Mamie became her mother's chief assistant there and in the library, while Jessie relieved her of some of the responsibilities of hospital matron. Maria was teaching at Fairmont Female College at Monteagle, Tennessee, an outgrowth of the school the Gorgas girls had attended while they lived at Sewanee. Richard Gorgas had received his degree from the University of Alabama in 1884. He studied medicine briefly before deciding to take a law degree, which he received in 1890.

The passing years in no way diminished Amelia's hospitable impulses. She kept in close touch with her sisters and her many nieces and nephews, and she welcomed their visits, writing Willie, "It is such a joy to me to be able to have the different members of the family visit me & to have a nice old house in which to accommodate them. I would be almost willing to give my services to the Univ. for the house alone." Her children were solicitous of her health and often urged her to go to "the Springs," but she preferred to remain in her quiet home and welcome those who would visit her there.

Sarah Crawford, who was suffering from severe arthritis, came with her daughter Millie in the summer of 1886; Amelia wrote Willie proudly that since their arrival Sarah had steadily improved and walked around the yard with crutches and that Millie looked like a different person.

Willie's October birthday was always a special occasion for Amelia whether he could be at home or not. The day after his birthday in 1886 she wrote:

> All day yesterday I was thinking of you & trying to get leisure to send you birthday greetings. Aunt Sarah also remembered the day & brought to the dinner table a bottle of champagne in which all drank to your health, long life & *numerous progeny*—My idea of happiness however does not include the last named—a moderate family is more desirable unless one has a settled home & a good old mammie nurse as existed in the good old "befoe-de-war-days"—But tell Marie we will accept the gifts the Gods send us without murmuring.[10]

Ties with friends of the past remained strong. In the spring of 1887, Colonel Mallet, who was still teaching at the University of Virginia, wrote Amelia that his children were coming to Tuscaloosa to visit their aunt and that he particularly wanted them to see her. He recalled with pleasure the days at Brierfield when the children were young. Perhaps Mallet felt as did another father, who sent his three young daughters to see Mrs. Gorgas so that they might learn how to grow old beautifully and be even more charming in age than in youth.[11]

Amelia was persuaded to leave home occasionally in spite of her protests against travel. She paid a visit to the Baynes and Mary Aiken in New Orleans in February 1888 and returned to Louisiana with Jessie in June of that year to be with Minnie, whose third child had arrived prematurely. The tiny girl was so frail that little hope was held for her survival, but she gained strength rapidly after the first few days. Amelia wrote Mamie that she had rolled the baby "in flannel and a down pillow & the bag of hot water to keep its blood circulating." The infant was named Amelia Gayle for her grand-mother and soon became known as Minna.

On her return to Tuscaloosa Amelia found that the trustees of the University had increased her salary by $100. She wrote Willie that the vote was given "*standing*—a mark of high honor they say."[12] At the same time the trustees voted an appropriation "for an electric light plant to take the place of gas in lighting the barracks and other public buildings." Three new faculty residences were authorized at a cost of $4000 each.[13] Most of the faculty lived on the campus, and they were a close community.

In 1889 Maria Gorgas decided to give up teaching and go to New York to study nursing, a choice that probably pleased Amelia very much. Her old friend Dr. Polk, who was still practicing in New York, encouraged and advised Maria as he had her brother during his medical school days. Willie was now at Fort Barrancas at Pensacola and had requested this assignment because of his continu-ing interest in the cause and treatment of yellow fever. This city like so many other coastal areas was the scene of numerous epidemics.

His wife Marie went from Pensacola to Tuscaloosa for the birth of their daughter, Aileen Lyster, on September 10, 1889. It was a proud day for William Crawford Gorgas, who was almost as old as his father had been at the time of his (Willie's) birth. Marie's desire to have her child born in Tuscaloosa strengthened the bonds between her and her mother-in-law. Amelia adored little Aileen, whose presence lured the avowed stay-at-home grandmother to Fort Barroncas several times during Dr. Gorgas's tour of duty there.

The passing years brought Amelia many painful breaks with the past. President Clayton, whom Amelia had admired very much, died in October 1889. His death was followed in December by that of Jefferson Davis. Even more distressing to her was the death of Thomas Bayne in New Orleans in 1891. He had been a tower of strength to his wife's three widowed sisters, and Amelia mourned him especially for his love and devotion to her husband. Shortly before his death Bayne had presented the University with a portrait of General Gorgas and the State of Alabama with one of Governor Gayle.

At sixty-five Amelia herself remained vigorous and active. The new University president, Richard Channing Jones, reported to the trustees in 1892:

> Members of the Corps of Cadets frequent the Library every day, and read useful books and articles in periodicals, many of which are read by them at the suggestion of Mrs. Gorgas, our estimable and accomplished librarian. It would be gratifying to anyone who feels an interest in the young men of Alabama to observe the refining influence which she exerts over the students in the University....[14]

Maria's career brought a new world into her mother's ken. After completing her training, she stayed in New York to care for Amelia Lyon, one of the daughters of her father's friend and supporter Francis Strother Lyon. Dr. Polk, who was Miss Lyon's brother-in-law, attended Miss Lyon and inspired Maria to write her mother, "He is the only Dr. I know who inspires me with unwavering confidence.... He is such a noble looking man, with all his intellectual & physical strength so kind & soothing in the sick room."

Maria's next position was that of nurse-companion to Mary Leroy King, the daughter of Mrs. Edward King of Newport, Rhode Island. Miss King was a semi-invalid, whose doctors recommended European travel for her health. Maria accompanied "Miss Mary" and her mother to London, Paris, Cannes, Zurich, and many popular health spas. Mrs. King gave Maria many opportunities to enjoy the places they visited, and Maria sent her mother fascinating descriptions of the world of wealth in which she moved. Amelia, who never had an opportunity to go to Europe, wrote, "I feel almost as if I had accompanied you in your delightful jaunts."[15] She must have been fascinated by Maria's account of the Paris wedding of Mrs. King's niece, Edith Dresser, to George Vanderbilt in June 1898:

> The Vanderbilt-Dresser wedding was perfect in every detail, & we were all present, Mrs. Gair & I having seats inside the ribbons—no wedding was ever more perfectly planned & carried out, largely due to Miss Dresser, the eldest sister, who has talent for that sort of thing—We all drove to the church from the Hotel in a fine landau, the courier on the box seat, wearing the regulation Prince Albert coat, top hat & white kid gloves. Mr. V's family sat on the right side of the aisle, & Miss Edith's on the left, & such beautiful dresses! & jewels! Americans who are gowned, coiffeured & millinered in Paris are simply perfect. Miss Mary was lovely in a pearl corded silk trimmed with soft tulle, white hat with black & white ostrich plumes & filled in with pink roses at the back. Her hair had been beautifully waved & dressed by a male hair-dresser (abominable creatures) just to suit the hat, & she looked tip-top. . . . Mrs. King wore a handsome black silk covered with steel paillettes, & she looked very well & was given the seat of honor—The four Dresser sisters, the shortest one being 5 ft. 8 in., were magnificent. The brother is 6 ft. 4 in. Miss Edith looked small beside him. She looked an Empress, high-necked white dress, very long train, veil, flowers, no jewels, & a splendid piece of lace which her mother & sisters wore at their weddings. . . .[16]

During the years Maria was with the Kings, she was able to come home for occasional visits. On one such visit she assisted in planning a course of study for the nurses at Bryce Hospital with special emphasis on the care of the insane.[17]

As Amelia grew older she cherished her memories of the Confederacy. She decided to go and "be one of the Veterans" at a reunion of Confederate Veterans in Birmingham in April 1894. She thoroughly enjoyed the occasion. "Every one[-]armed & one[-]legged confederate brought tears to my eyes and the old 'rebel yell' thrilled through and through my faithful heart," she wrote Maria. "General Shoup & I could scarcely resist an embrace in public & he declared I was younger & more active than at Sewanee." She was one of the charter

members of the R. E. Rodes Chapter of the United Daughters of the
Confederacy, which was organized in Tuscaloosa in May 1896. She
clipped many poems lamenting the Confederate dead and read Fitz-
hugh Lee's life of his uncle, Robert E. Lee, with tears in her eyes,
recalling as she did the sad partings the night Richmond was evacuated and her inconsolable grief when the news of Lee's surrender
was brought to Richmond by some half-clad and half-starved young
officers. "Not many are left to grieve over those dark days," she said,
"and I believe I rather enjoy an occasional indulgence in the harrow-
ing reminiscences."[18]

The last five years of the nineteenth century found Amelia an
important personage in the life of the University of Alabama. In
June 1895 the *Atlanta Constitution* printed an article entitled "Story
of the University of Alabama." One paragraph headed "A Good
Mother to the Boys" read:

> A very important place in a sketch of the university for many years
> past belongs to Mrs. Gorgas, the venerable and estimable librarian
> and hospital matron. . . . Mrs. Gorgas has a warm friend in every
> university boy for there are few to whom her kindly hands have not
> administered. Her gentle voice and her beautiful snow white hair are
> indelibly impressed upon the memories of her former patients and
> charges—the boys of Alabama.[19]

The University yearbook, *The Corolla*, for 1896 was dedicated to
Amelia in the following words:

DEDICAMUS

Conforming to the unanimous desire of the ALABAMA CADET CORPS,
and
thus, in a measure, expressing their filial love,
THE COROLLA OF 1896
is dedicated to
* * * MRS. AMELIA G. GORGAS, * * *
whose tender ministrations to the sick, motherly counsel to the way-
ward and erring, and words of encouragement and
incentive to all, have made her the good
angel of their college home.

In an "Editorial" the student editor of the yearbook wrote in honor of the seventy-year-old librarian:

> Recognizing the influences for good upon us all of that which is truest and noblest, a Southern Woman, and knowing that the highest type is combined in "OUR LIBRARIAN," Mrs. Amelia G. Gorgas, who has been to us always tender, thoughtful, unselfish—a mother— to her, the most revered and beloved person of the University, we dedicate this our best efforts.

A copy of the book was sent to Millie Crawford inscribed: "Amelia G. Crawford / from her Aunt Amelia G. Gorgas / University 1896 / Tuscaloosa—Alabama.[20]

In these years of public acclaim Amelia was still much occupied with her family. In the late summer of 1894 Jessie had written Willie: "We are making a great stir in the house preparing for Aunt Sarah's coming, will put her in the parlor and move the parlor furniture to the downstairs room.... Her longing to get back to Alabama is intense and a note from her tonight very pathetic." Sarah and Millie had been living in Edgefield, South Carolina, with Sarah's daughter Sallie, her son-in-law Samuel Hughes, and their three children. Sarah was now so crippled by arthritis that Richard Gorgas had to meet her in Atlanta, accompany her to Tuscaloosa, and bring her to the Gorgas home in an ambulance. A week after her arrival Amelia wrote Maria that Sarah was better than she had dared to hope, though she was unable even to sit up in bed.[21]

Amelia planned to have a visit from her granddaughter Aileen while Willie and Marie went north that fall. They must have written Amelia that they feared the child would be too much for her with Sarah ill in the house, for Amelia wrote Marie:

> I will never forgive you if you do not leave my baby Aileen here with us when you go North.
> She will be the greatest pleasure & no trouble in the world—Sarah . . . loves to have the little children of the neighborhood in her room when they come to ask after her—She & Millie occupy the parlor in which we placed her handsome old furniture & the noises of the house & of the post office do not reach her though she is not at all disturbed by

noise. . . . She came to Tus. to die, but declares without any fault of her own she is afraid she is getting well. Millie too looks better far, than I expected, all the effect she says of her cheerful surroundings. All this makes me very happy & thankful but I shall be very unhappy if Sarah's presence deprives me of my babys visit.

If the tricycle is not hopelessly broken do send it up by freight, she can ride on the hard roads around the campus & she will be the wonder of the lookers on—. . .[22]

Sarah and Millie remained in Tuscaloosa for more than a year as beloved members of the family. Even Amelia's devoted nursing could not cure Sarah's illness, but faculty friends, visitors from Mobile, and acquaintances in town were attentive to her and helped make the long days of suffering easier to bear. However, late in October 1895, word came that her little granddaughter Sarah Crawford Hughes had been burned to death, and the blow seemed more than she could bear. She died on November 29. Amelia accompanied Millie to Mobile for the funeral and interment in the family plot in Magnolia Cemetery. Amelia and Mary Aiken, whose own poor health kept her from attending the funeral, were now the only survivors of John and Sarah Gayle's six children. Richard Gayle had died in 1873 and Matthew in 1875.

The beginning of the Spanish American War in April 1898 brought new duties and opportunities to Willie, who at forty-four was still "My darling boy" to his mother. He had been ordered to New York City in the preceding December but was soon transferred to a hospital ship, then to a yellow-fever hospital in Siboney, Cuba. Amelia wrote him in May 1898 that the war seemed "far-away & unreal to this old-Confederate woman" and added that there was no exhibition of patriotism whatever in her part of the country and that the officers had found it difficult to fill the companies of the state troops and impossible to enlist recruits. She continued, "We shall have no guests during Commencement & I always enjoy meeting the old boys & the politicians who gather here at that time—Bishop Gailor, your old friend, preaches the Commencement sermon & I regret I have no room to offer him but I will manage to give him a glass of iced claret before & after the sermon."[23]

Seriously ill in the late summer, Dr. Gorgas planned a trip home in the fall to recuperate. His mother wrote:

In anticipation of your coming & remembering your inherited tastes we have succeeded in getting a fat old time cook—who is said to excel in frying chickens & making batter bread—Marie & Jessie will contribute salads so you shall be fed to your hearts desire if only your "Siboney stomach" will permit.

Richie writes that he will get a two days leave & join our happy family circle. Minnie & George would not be allowed to enter Tuscaloosa, so abject is the fear of these inland towns, of yellow fever—Minnie continues well though the fever is all around them but of so light a type they do not in the least fear it—[24]

Amelia welcomed her grandchildren as warmly as she did her children. Minna Palfrey was with her grandmother when Willie, Marie, and Aileen visited that fall, and Aileen remained during the winter and spring while her mother accompanied her father back to Cuba to begin the task that was to make his reputation for generations to come. Jessie Palfrey, who had spent a great deal of time in Tuscaloosa through the years, attended the University as a special student in 1899.[25] Writing Willie just before the close of the school year, Amelia said, "I hope no changes will be made this year—though a feeling of uncertainty prevails more or less at every meeting of the trustees. Happy are officers of the Army & Navy who are secure in their positions unless killed by Phillipinos or Cubans. I am a traitor in admiring the courage of Aguinaldo who will be counted as a great rebel as was Washington and Lee."[26] Professors at the University had to be reappointed every year by the trustees. Army life looked better to Amelia now than it had when she and Josiah had tried so hard to discourage Willie in his attempt to go to West Point.

A pleasant change was made in the appearance of Amelia's campus home late in the 1890s. As a birthday gift to Mrs. Gorgas a former professor and friend, Benjamin Hardaway, designed a new portico. Two archways were added, one on either side of the original one, and the cast-iron stairs that curved down from the upper entrance were moved apart. As advancing years began to restrict Mrs. Gorgas's activities, there was ample opportunity for enjoyment of the two porches provided by the new arrangement.

RETIREMENT AT EIGHTY

When William Crawford Gorgas, now Major Gorgas, went to Cuba in 1898 to combat yellow fever, the cause of the disease was still unknown. The mosquito theory of transmission was as yet propounded by only a few scientists. Gorgas himself rejected the theory and with the members of his staff went to work to clean up the city of Havana. It was a tremendous task, but a thorough job was done. However, though the general health improved and other diseases were greatly reduced in number, yellow fever was not affected. The number of cases even increased. The surgeon-general sent a board of army medical officers, headed by Major Walter Reed, to Cuba to see what could be done. Major Reed's experiments, based on research by Dr. Carlos Finlay, Dr. Henry R. Carter, and others resulted in the knowledge that the disease was indeed transmitted by the mosquito, specifically, *Aedes (Stegomyia) aegypti*. Once this fact was established, it became Major Gorgas's task to decide how to go about combating the insect. Vaccination against its bite had not proved effective, and efforts to isolate patients in the early days of the disease were not successful because of the difficulty of diagnosing it quickly. It became evident that the mosquito itself would have to be destroyed.

With the knowledge that the yellow-fever mosquito usually inhabited a rather limited area and that all mosquitoes go through a larval stage when they must live in water, Gorgas felt that collections of water were vital areas. He learned that the yellow-fever mosquito, unlike other mosquitoes, preferred the water in artificial containers found around homes to natural pools and ponds. This mosquito not only liked man-made containers for its water but also preferred to have human beings around. It would not use the cisterns at an unoccupied house but moved in as soon as people did.

Armed with this information, Gorgas began his attack. New regulations required all rainwater receptacles to be covered, and carpenters paid out of public funds helped citizens prepare their rain barrels and cisterns properly. Kerosene poured on the surface of water collecting in gutters and similar places proved effective, for the larvae would suffocate when they drew the oil into their breathing tubes. Indoor breeding places were harder for Gorgas's men to eliminate, for inevitably many citizens resented rules that interfered with their privacy and the routine of their daily lives. A great measure of Gorgas's success in overcoming this resentment was the result of his gentle manner, his tact, and his persuasiveness, all qualities that had helped his mother over many of the difficult times in her life. His office was always open to those with grievances, and he would patiently explain the need for his regulations.[1]

Amelia was deeply interested in all that her son was doing. She wrote him, "The Havana papers and the 'monthly statistics' keep me quite in touch with you and your big work." She added that Dr. Polk's wife had written of their pleasure in the complimentary notice the press was taking of his work: "We have always had a weak spot in our hearts for him and feel very sure he deserves all if not more than is said. Do give our love and congratulations."[2] Another trait Dr. Gorgas shared with his mother was the gift of making friends for life.

Willie and Marie urged Amelia to visit them in Cuba in 1901, but the thought of even a short sea voyage "appalled" her. She wrote Willie later that year that she preferred to remain in the "rest and repose" of her comfortable home: "I shall pose as the 'mountain' to which my Mahomets must come in at least a yearly pilgrimage."[3]

Dr. Gorgas's work in Havana was almost complete. The last case of yellow fever was recorded on September 26, 1901. His success in combating malaria in Cuba was also a great achievement and one for which its citizens had reason to be grateful. He left Havana in the fall of 1902 and after a few months in Washington was sent to

Governor's Island, New York. In March 1903 he was promoted to
colonel by an act of Congress as recognition of his work in Cuba. He
wrote his mother:

> This, of course, is a great honor for me. It is the first time an Army
> Medical officer has been directly recognized by Congress. It places
> me in a rank that would have taken me about 15 years to reach in the
> ordinary course of promotion and increases my pay eighty dollars per
> month. Mr. Bankhead had nominal charge of the bill & did all he
> could.[4] I went around to thank him the other day and he said all that
> you can do for me in return is just tell your Mother that I helped all I
> could—that I did my very best as some return for her kindness to my
> boy when he was at the University. Senator Pettus introduced the bill
> and pushed it through the Senate. I went to thank him the other day.
> He said now young man I am glad to have been able to assist you but
> what I did was for your grandfather, your Mother and your Father's
> sake. His grandnephew who is at the University now writes that you
> have been very kind to him.[5]

Although Amelia had celebrated her seventy-fifth birthday in
June 1901, she continued to work regularly in the University library
through yet another change in administration. James Knox Powers
had succeeded General Richard C. Jones as president in 1897 and
served until 1901. When he resigned, Dr. Wyman finally agreed to
accept the presidency, having served as acting president several
times in the past. Amelia wrote Willie, "The election of Prof.
Wyman as Pres. of the University gives the most general satisfaction
over the state & is especially gratifying to me. We are old & intimate
friends & I anticipate a successful year for the University & an
agreeable one for myself."[6]

In August 1903 Amelia and Mamie visited Willie and Marie on
Governor's Island. Amelia watched the ships in New York Harbor
and planned to do as much sight-seeing as her strength would permit, but when Dr. Polk wanted to take her to drive in his au-
tomobile, she said that she was timid about "these new-fangled
things" and wrote Maria that she hoped she would be allowed to
decline. She also wrote her daughter, "I hope Mrs. Jefferson Davis is
in the City as I greatly desire to see her once again. She & Mrs. Clay
Clopton [the former Mrs. Clement Clay who had traveled south

with Josiah in 1866] & myself are among the last remaining of the Confederate women & we feel close to each other."[7]

From New York Amelia and Mamie went to Washington where Richard was now working. Here they met Josiah's great niece, Kate Brooks, who was music critic and society reporter for the Washington *Post*. She gave them a package of letters Josiah had written to his mother when he was a young man. While in Washington Amelia was taken to see the Adams Monument, sometimes called "The Peace of God" or "Grief," by Augustus Saint-Gaudens. She returned several times to Rock Creek Park Cemetery to look at the monument, which she found very moving. Mamie called her mother's trip a "triumphal march," and Amelia said, "Surely no woman every enjoyed it so much & no mother was ever blessed with such dear children solicitous & tender for my comfort."[8]

Willie was soon to undertake a task that would fill his mother with even greater pride in him. From the start of negotiations for building the Panama Canal, he had expressed his hope of being involved in the project, and in March 1904 he began his work as chief sanitary officer. He wrote his sister Maria in August: "The work is a great work and very attractive to me though I am very much discouraged at starting. The Commission have their own ideas of sanitation and do not seem impressed by mine." In spite of the success of his methods in Cuba, there were many in high positions in the government who still refused to believe that the mosquito and not filth was the cause of yellow fever. Gorgas's struggles to get the support he needed make a long story of frustration before his efforts were finally successful.[9]

The summer her son began his work in Panama, Amelia celebrated her seventy-eighth birthday and admitted that age was beginning to tell on her. "No one who knew me in the days gone by can imagine how completely I have lost all energy & capacity for writing. I make no explanation for I do not understand it myself only I feel unable to do anything beyond the few daily duties devolving upon me." She looked forward, however, to having the Palfreys with her for the summer and spoke with interest of the summer school which the University would be opening on June 14: "Beside the regular lessons there is to be a lecture every evening at 5 o'clock

& an attendance of 4 or 500 men & women are expected—all this will brighten the campus & I dare say afford some amusement to lookers on."

Her unfailing interest in her work and in her family continued to give meaning to her days. In August 1904 she sent a birthday message to Maria, who was remaining temporarily with Mrs. King after "Miss Mary's" death in January: "Maybe this will reach you on the 4th bearing from your old Mother more love than one small sheet can contain. But I want you to know, my child, what joy & strength you impart to me whether present or absent. You and Willie possess the same supreme faith and happy belief in the future which takes the pangs from parting."[10] She shared with Maria her worries about Jessie's poor health and about Richard's life without a family to look after him, and she spoke of giving up university life in the coming year to make a little home for him somewhere.

Her retirement was, however, still two years away. At the commencement exercises in June 1905 the University alumni presented her with a silver loving cup, and she allowed her photograph to be taken for one of the few times in her life. The Tuscaloosa *Times Gazette* described the presentation:

> Directly after the address of the Hon. James Weatherly of Birmingham, Mr. Ferguson announced that a loving cup would be presented to Mrs. Gorgas, the universally beloved librarian of the University by the alumni. The presentation speech was made by the Hon. T. M. Owen, of Montgomery, and as he spoke of the deep love and reverence every student who has ever attended the University felt for her, his voice showed his feeling which was echoed in every heart present and many an old student as he thought of the sick bed made less grievous by her tender ministration and the sweet and gentle influence she had wielded over his college life felt the tears well up in his eyes. It was a moment fraught with precious memories. For twenty-five years Mrs. Gorgas has been librarian. . . .
>
> The cup is a large sterling silver affair of beautiful workmanship and if it had been big enough to hold all the love of the alumni, Clark Hall could not have held it.[11]

Another article noted: "Although Mrs. Gorgas is very feeble she acquitted herself in the sweet womanly manner that has endeared her to thousands of the boys and men of Alabama."[12] It gave Amelia added pleasure to have her only grandson, Taylor Palfrey, take his degree from the University at this commencement.

At the 1906 graduation exercises the University celebrated its seventy-fifth anniversary. Amelia wrote Minnie that she sat in the library and "welcomed as many of the old alumni as I could remember—... everyone made much of me & I was a proud old woman." Major Fairbanks, who had been such a good friend to her and to Josiah at Sewanee, was there for the ceremonies. She wrote that he "looked as well & almost as active as a man of 60. I enjoyed so meeting him—" Fairbanks presented Amelia and the University library with copies of his recently published history of the University of the South.

Following the anniversary celebration, Amelia, Jessie, and Maria, who had now retired and come home to live, went to Christiansburg, Virginia, where they enjoyed the mountain air in a comfortable boarding house. Amelia wrote her daughter-in-law from Virginia and in her letter quoted a poignant passage from a letter from Mary Aiken, whose life had held so much sadness: "It seems to me your life has rounded out perfectly. Your children are all living & your eldest son, the idol of your heart, has attained a reputation which makes him one of the most distinguished men of the country. You have had many trials but the end of your life is blessed."[13]

During the fall of 1906 a movement was started to secure for Mrs. Gorgas a pension from the Carnegie Foundation, which would reward her faithful service and enable her to retire with some degree of security. A pension of $750 a year was awarded her, and she finally retired on January 1, 1907, at the age of eighty.[14] The trustees of the University gave her the privilege of renting, for a nominal sum, the house that had been her home for so long, and retirement thus brought about no radical change in her way of life. Mamie Gorgas was to continue on the library staff.

In her years of retirement Amelia Gorgas followed her son's work in Panama and rejoiced in the acclaim he received from many sources. He sent her a clipping from the *Boston Transcript* that read:

Every man who has been in the fever ward swears by Colonel Gorgas. Although at the head of one of the largest and busiest departments and obliged to be at his office in the city most of the day, he visits personally everyone in the fever ward morning and evening and prescribes for their treatment. Not a man among them who does not feel 100 per cent better after his visits. He has a wonderfully attractive personality, is equally kind and courteous to the humblest and above all inspires an implicit confidence in his treatment which removes all worry from the patient's mind and makes very strongly for his recovery. . . . Many a man has been heard to say that it was worth having the yellow fever to have been under the care of Colonel Gorgas.[15]

William Crawford Gorgas received honorary degrees from a number of universities, including his alma mater, the University of the South. In 1904 he made the commencement address there. In May 1907 he received the Mary Kingsley medal of the Liverpool School of Tropical Medicine, and in June 1908 he wrote his mother from Chicago of his election as president of the American Medical Association. His visit to Tuscaloosa later that summer filled his proud mother's cup to overflowing. He was awarded an honorary LL.D. degree by the University of Alabama in 1910, and when the University offered him its presidency in 1911, he expressed his "acute" regret at having to decline a position so attractive to him, saying that every consideration of sentiment and affection bound him to Alabama, but that his duty lay in Panama until the canal was finished.[16]

Amelia's devoted children and admiring friends filled her last years with all the love and care with which she had blessed them for so long. One of Willie's last letters to her closed, "A love & a kiss for my dear Mother and a grateful recollection of 58 years of love, patience and never changing affection."[17] He said later that his mother's most remarkable and lovable characteristic was the entire absence on her part of any idea that she was undergoing any particular self-sacrifice.

Amelia Gayle Gorgas died on the third of January 1913. With her were all her children except Willie, who was still in Panama. Her old friend Dr. Wyman was at her bedside at the end. He held her hand, saying: "She was a great lady. She was a very great lady."[18]

EPILOGUE

Mrs. Gorgas's funeral service was conducted in the auditorium of Morgan Hall on the University campus by the Reverend Edwin A. Penick, rector of Christ Episcopal Church in Tuscaloosa. Pallbearers included her old friends on the University faculty. Obituaries called her "one of the most widely known and beloved women that Alabama has ever claimed."

Before a month had passed, William B. Bankhead of Jasper, Alabama, soon to be elected to Congress, wrote a letter calling on alumni of the University to see that a suitable memorial be made to Mrs. Gorgas. A proposal for a memorial library soon followed. In May 1913 Dr. George H. Denny, president of the University, formally suggested, "as fitting memorial to this beloved woman, a great Gorgas Library."

Twelve years passed before the memorial became a reality, but in 1925 the Amelia Gorgas Memorial Library was opened. The building housed administrative offices on the ground floor with the library occupying the upper floors. This library served the students of the University until 1940, when the present Amelia Gayle Gorgas Library was built almost on the site of the original Rotunda, which had been destroyed during the Civil War. In 1937 a group of alumni presented the University with a portrait of Mrs. Gorgas, which now hangs in the Gorgas Library. At the same time a sketch of the life of Amelia Gayle Gorgas, written by Clara L. Verner, was published.

Mrs. Gorgas's daughters stayed in the campus home after their mother's death, and Mamie Gorgas continued to serve on the library staff. William Crawford Gorgas outlived his mother by only seven years. He served as surgeon general of the United States Army during World War I, retiring at the end of the war to accept an offer from the Rockefeller Foundation, which enabled him to return to his work in the eradication of yellow fever and other tropical diseases. He was taken ill in London in the summer of 1920 and died there on July 4. During his last illness he was visited by King George V, who presented him with the insigne of the Order of St. Michael and St. George.

Jessie Gorgas died in Tuscaloosa in 1925. Richard Gorgas, though youngest of the family was the next to go. He had served as a captain in World War I and continued in government service until his retirement in 1931. He died in Birmingham in 1935. Mamie Gorgas lived until 1944, dying at the age of eighty-six. In that same year, the Alabama State Legislature, largely through the efforts of the Alabama Federation of Women's Clubs, approved a measure establishing the Gorgas home as a historic site and a memorial to the Gorgas family. The Gorgas Memorial Board was formed to administer the property, and after the deaths of the last of the Gorgas children, Maria Gorgas and Minnie Palfrey (both in their nineties) in 1953, the house was restored and opened to the public. Visitors to the house can see many mementos of the Gorgas family on display there today.

NOTES

Chapter 1

1. William E. W. Yerby, *History of Greensboro, Alabama From Its Earliest Settlement* (Montgomery, Alabama: The Paragon Press, 1908), 2-15, 36-37.

2. Sarah H. Gayle, *Journal*, October 1827, MS in Gayle-Gorgas Collection, Amelia Gayle Gorgas Library, University of Alabama. Typescript belonging to George Tait, Richmond, Virginia. "My youngest darling bore, for three months, the name of Ellen, but when my friend died, with a thousand crowding emotions, I blotted it from the record & in its place wrote *Amelia Ross.*" Her friend Amelia Fisher had married Jack Ferrell Ross.

3. Willis Brewer, *Alabama: Her History, Resources, War Record, and Public Men From 1540 to 1872* (Montgomery, Alabama: Barrett and Brown, 1872), 402-03; also William Garrett, *Reminiscences of Public Men in Alabama for Thirty Years* (Atlanta, Georgia: Plantation Publishing Company's Press, 1872), 458-59. Albert Burton Moore, *History of Alabama and Her People*, 3 vols. (Chicago and New York: The American Historical Society, 1927), I, 141.

4. Yerby, *History of Greensboro*, 3-4, 36-37; Eastin had been Alabama's Territorial Printer.

5. Gayle, *Journal*, October 1827, March 5, April 13, 1828; Greensboro (Alabama) *Watchman*, January 1942.

6. Gayle, *Journal*, Extracts on Amelia Gayle copied from the *Journal* and in the Gayle-Gorgas Collection, Amelia Gayle Gorgas Library, University of Alabama, (hereafter cited as GGC).

7. Moore, *History of Alabama*, I, 216.

8. Sarah H. Gayle to John Gayle, December 17, 1831, January 9, 10, 1832, GGC.

9. Ibid., November 29, 1831.

10. Gayle, *Journal*, May 16, 1832, June 29, 1832, January 13, 1833.

11. Ewing's Tavern is preserved as "The Old Tavern" by the Tuscaloosa County Preservation Society.

12. Sarah H. Gayle to Mrs. Mary Peck, April 16, 1833, April 28, 1834, May 17, 1835, GGC.

13. Gayle, *Journal*, December 15, 1833; see also Thomas Chalmers McCorvey, *Alabama Historical Sketches* (Charlottesville, Virginia: University of Virginia Press, 1960), 56-64.

14. Gayle, *Journal*, February 21, 1834.

15. Sarah H. Gayle to Mrs. Mary Peck, April 28, 1834, GGC.

16. Gayle, *Journal*, March 16, 1834, May [June] 1, 1834.

17. Ibid., February 19,1831.

18. Sarah H. Gayle to Mrs. Mary Peck, October 1833, GGC.

19. Charles Grayson Summersell, *Historical Foundations of Mobile* (University, Alabama: University of Alabama Press, 1949), 12, 21.

20. Manuscript in Sarah Gayle Crawford's scrapbook owned by her granddaughter, Mary Adams Hughes, of Edgefield, South Carolina.

21. Sarah H. Gayle to John Gayle, July 4, 1835, Hughes Collection.

22. *Extracts From The Journal of Sarah Haynesworth Gayle* (New Rochelle, New York: The Knickerbocker Press, 1895), 7.

23. Amelia Gayle Gorgas Scrapbook owned by George Tait, Richmond, Virginia; Letters in GGC; Sarah Gayle Crawford, *Journal*, June 27, 1849, GGC.

Chapter 2

1. James B. Sellers, *History of the University of Alabama, 1818–1902*, Vol. I, (University, Alabama: University of Alabama Press, 1953), 30–34, 56, 58.

2. Gayle, *Journal*, December 25, 1834; William R. Smith, Sr., *Reminiscences of A Long Life*, Vol. I (Washington, D.C.: William R. Smith, Sr., 1889), 207; Crawford, *Journal*, June 27, 1849.

3. Edwin S. Craighead and Frank Craighead, *Craighead's Mobile*, ed. Caldwell Delaney (Mobile: The Haunted Bookshop, 1968), 108; Richard N. Current, T. Harry Williams, and Frank Freidel, *American History: A Survey* (New York: Alfred A. Knopf, 1961), 259–60.

4. Crawford, *Journal*, August 5, 1839.

5. Madame Canda's husband was Charles Canda, listed in the New York City Directory, 1840–41 as "Art Teacher" at 17 LaFayette.

6. Moultrie Guerry, *Men Who Made Sewanee* (Sewanee, Tennessee: University Press, 1932), 6.

7. Amelia Gayle to Sarah Gayle, August 24, 1841, GGC.

8. Matthew Gayle to William B. Crawford, August 10, 1842, Hughes Collection.

9. Amelia Gayle to Sarah Gayle Crawford, July 25, 1843, GGC.

10. Mary Crawford Marmaduke to Jessie Gorgas, January 2, 1916, Tait Collection.

11. *Craighead's Mobile*, 49.

12. In an excerpt from a letter from Mrs. Elizabeth Swepstone Heustis to

Richard Whitehead Gayle, February 18, 1848, is: "Cousin John is a member of Congress and is now in Washington City. Amelia went with him. Clara and her two children are in Greensboro, boarding until his return next June...." (Clara Gayle's two children were Frederick, born in 1843, and Helen, born in 1846.) Tait Collection.

Chapter 3

1. *Richmond Whig and Public Advertiser*, November 30, 1847.
2. W. H. Parmalee, "Recollections of an Old Stager," *Harper's New Monthly Magazine*, XLVII (1873), 757. See also Margaret L. Coit, *John C. Calhoun, American Patriot* (Boston: Houghton Mifflin Co., 1950), 343.
3. Ishbel Ross, *First Lady of the South: The Life of Mrs. Jefferson Davis* (New York: Harper and Brothers, 1958), 30; Sarah Mytton Maury, *Statesmen of America in 1846* (Philadelphia: Carey and Hart, 1847), 168.
4. Amelia Gayle to Sarah Crawford, March 29, 1848, GGC. See also description of Amelia Gayle in account written by Richard Gorgas, Tait Collection.
5. Holman Hamilton, *Zachary Taylor: Soldier in the White House* (Indianapolis and New York: Bobbs-Merrill Co., 1951), 66.
6. Accounts written by Richard Gorgas and Thomas Bragg, Tait Collection; Coit, *John C. Calhoun*, gives a version of this story, 485.
7. Maury, *Statesmen of America*, 128.
8. Amelia Gayle to Sarah Crawford, March 29, 1848, GGC.
9. Sketches of the Debates and Proceedings of the First Session of the Thirtieth Congress, *Congressional Globe* (Washington: Blair and Rives, 1848), 542.
10. Amelia Gayle to Matthew Gayle, April 23, 1848, GGC.
11. Garrett, *Reminiscences*, 474.
12. Amelia Gayle to Sarah Crawford, March 29–April 1, 1848, GGC.
13. Amelia Gayle to Matthew Gayle, April 23, 1848, GGC.
14. Clipping in Amelia Gayle Gorgas Scrapbook, Tait Collection.
15. "History of the Washington Monument," *Senate Documents* No. 224, 1902–1903, XXI, 45; "Our Capital," ibid., No. 13, 1955, I, 41.

Chapter 4

1. John Y. Mason to Amelia Gayle, September 2, 1848, Amelia Gayle Gorgas Scrapbook, Tait Collection.

2. Garrett, *Reminiscences*, 511.

3. Anne Gayle was the daughter of John Gayle's brother, Levin, who died in 1847.

4. Mary Crawford Marmaduke to Jessie Gorgas, January 2, 1916, Tait Collection.

5. Clara, Amelia (Millie), and William B., Jr.

6. Crawford, *Journal*, May 2, 31, June 2, 1849, GGC. Truman Smith was congressman for Connecticut.

7. Crawford, *Journal*, June 27, August 5, 12, 1849.

8. Mrs. Elizabeth Swepstone Gayle Heustis to Richard Whitehead Gayle, Mobile, February 18,1848, Copy in Tait Collection.

9. *Mobile Daily Register*, March 30, 1850; Joseph Leach, *Bright Particular Star: The Life and Times of Charlotte Cushman* (New Haven and London: Yale University Press, 1970), 228–29.

10. *Mobile Daily Register*, April 1, 1850.

11. Christopher Hollis, *The American Heresy* (New York: Minton, Balch & Co., 1930), 143.

12. *Mobile Daily Register*, June 4, 1859. See also James F. Sulzby, Jr., *Historic Alabama Hotels and Resorts* (University, Alabama: University of Alabama Press, 1960).

13. Crawford, *Journal*, July 17, August 1, September 10, 1853.

14. Thomas McAdory Owen, "A Bibliography of Alabama," *Annual Report of the American Historical Association for the Year 1897* (Washington: Government Printing Office, 1898), 1092.

15. Marie D. Gorgas and Burton J. Hendrick, *William Crawford Gorgas, His Life and Work* (Garden City, New York: Doubleday, Page and Co., 1924), 23.

16. Frank E. Vandiver, *Ploughshares Into Swords: Josiah Gorgas and Confederate Ordnance* (Austin: University of Texas Press, 1952), 3–36.

17. Ibid., 36; Josiah Gorgas to Col. H. K. Craig, June 30, July 9, 1853, Ordnance Records, letters received by the Chief of Ordnance, 1853, File G, Docs. 82, 88.

18. GGC.

19. Crawford, *Journal*, September 13, 20, 21, October 8, 16, 1853.

20. William B. Crawford to John Gayle, September 1853, Hughes Collection.

21. Crawford, *Journal*, October 22, November 10, 1853.

Chapter 5

1. Crawford, *Journal*, December 8, 1853; Dr. Nott wrote to Dr. Crawford giving this figure.

2. Marriage Certificate, *Register of Christ Church*, Mobile, II, 238, copy, GGC; Mary Crawford Marmaduke to Jessie Gorgas, January 2, 1916, Tait Collection.

3. Mrs. Gorgas recalled many years later the wild drive from the Mobile and Ohio Railroad to Mt. Vernon behind four span of army mules (Clipping in Amelia Gayle Gorgas Scrapbook).

4. "Epistolary Gossipings of Travel, Etc.," *Russell's Magazine*, May 1859, 134–35. See also Frank E. Vandiver, "The Authorship of Certain Contributions to Russell's Magazine," *Georgia Historical Quarterly*, XXXI (1947), 118–20.

5. Vandiver, *Ploughshares Into Swords*, 38.

6. Richard Gayle had resigned his commission in the Navy June 1853, and was temporarily back in Mobile.

7. Amelia Gorgas to Sarah Crawford, April 23, 1854, GGC.

8. Josiah Gorgas to Amelia Gorgas, December 15, 1854, GGC.

Chapter 6

1. Josiah Gorgas, *Journal*, January 12, March 6, 1857, MS GGC.

2. Gorgas, *Journal*, January 1, 12, 28, March 17, 1857.

3. Ibid., June 30, 1857.

4. Mary Gayle Aiken to Hugh Kerr Aiken, November 16, 1857; Manuscript in Gayle-Aiken Papers, South Caroliniana Library, University of South Carolina.

5. Gorgas, *Journal*, December 13, 1857, April 29, June 1, 1858.

6. Amelia Gorgas to Josiah Gorgas, May 30, June 2, 6, July 15, 23, 1858, GGC.

7. Josiah Gorgas to Amelia Gorgas, Monday morning [July 1858], Amelia Gorgas to Josiah Gorgas, June 27, July 4, 1858, GGC.

8. Mary Gayle Aiken to Hugh Kerr Aiken, August 16, 1858, Gayle-Aiken Papers, South Caroliniana Library.

9. Amelia Gorgas to Josiah Gorgas, June 11, 18, 27, 1858, Josiah Gorgas to Amelia Gorgas, July 7, 17, August 1, 1858, GGC.

10. Mr. Fessenden was senator from Maine.

11. Amelia Gorgas to Josiah Gorgas, June 27, 1858, GGC.

12. Vandiver, *Ploughshares Into Swords*, 47. Gorgas to Craig, July 9, 1858, Ordnance Records, letters received by Chief of Ordnance, 1858, File G, Doc. 149.

13. Amelia Gorgas to Josiah Gorgas, July 15, 1858, GGC; Hudson Strode, *Jefferson Davis, American Patriot 1808–1861* (New York: Harcourt, Brace and Co., 1955), 306–07.

14. Vandiver, *Ploughshares Into Swords*, 47. Gorgas to Craig, July 9, 1858,

Ordnance Records, letters received by the Chief of Ordnance, 1858, Doc. 149.

15. Josiah Gorgas to Amelia Gorgas, July 17, 1858, Amelia Gorgas to Josiah Gorgas, July 23, 1858, GGC.

16. Gorgas, *Journal*, July 25, 1858.

17. Vandiver, *Ploughshares Into Swords*, 49.

Chapter 7

1. Amelia Gorgas to Josiah Gorgas, June 11, 1858, GGC.

2. Mrs. Rhett died in June 1860, before the Gorgas family left Charleston. Josiah Gorgas, *Journal*, July 1, 1860.

3. The editor was Paul Hamilton Hayne.

4. Gorgas, *Journal*, May 24, July 4, October 28, 1859.

5. Ibid., April 25, June 3, 1860.

6. Ibid., March 31, 1861.

7. Vandiver, *Ploughshares Into Swords*, 53–54. See also note 39, p. 54.

8. Gorgas, *Journal*, March 31, 1861.

Chapter 8

1. Gorgas and Hendrick, *William Crawford Gorgas*, 34

2. *Daily Richmond Enquirer*, November 27, 1860.

3. Mary Henry Lyon.

4. During her first marriage to a Mr. Pope, Mrs. Randolph had resided in Mobile.

5. Mary H. Jones to Sarah Gayle Crawford, December 30, 1861, GGC.

6. Sallie A. Putnam, *In Richmond During the Confederacy by A Lady of Richmond* (New York: Robert M. McBride Co., 1961, Reprinted from the 1867 Edition), 112.

7. Charles Minnegerode to Amelia Gayle Gorgas, "Mrs. Col. Gorgas," May 6, 1862, GGC.

8. This Prayer Book may be seen at the Gorgas House on The University of Alabama campus.

9. Gorgas, *Journal*, July 27, 1862.

10. Thomas L. Bayne, *Autobiography* typescript 27–28, Bayne-Gayle Papers, Southern Historical Collection, University of North Carolina.

11. Josiah Gorgas to Amelia Gorgas, Sunday Eve. [July], August 3, Sunday, August, Wednesday, 1862, Sunday [1862, possibly October 12], GGC.

12. Robert Beverley Munford, Jr., *Richmond Homes and Memories* (Richmond, Virginia: Garrett and Massie, 1936), 14.

13. Gorgas, *Journal*, Saturday, March 21, March 25, May 3, 9, 13, 14, 1863.

14. J.P. Holcombe, lawyer, educator, member of the Confederate Congress; his farm was in Bedford County, *DAB*, IX, 134–35.

15. Mary Boykin Chesnut, *A Diary from Dixie* (Boston: Houghton Mifflin Co., 1949), 315. Mrs. Chesnut uses the spelling "Drury's Bluff."

16. Gorgas, *Journal*, September 3, October 29, November 11, 1863, January 10, 1864.

17. Chesnut, *Diary*, 350–51.

18. John R. Thompson was editor of *The Southern Literary Messenger;* Mary S. Preston was daughter of General and Mrs. John S. Preston of South Carolina. Thomas Cooper De Leon, *Belles, Beaux and Brains of the 60's* (New York: G. W. Dillingham Co., 1909), 232.

19. Clipping in Amelia Gayle Gorgas Scrapbook, Tait Collection.

20. Gorgas, *Journal*, March 23, 25 1864.

Chapter 9

1. Gorgas, *Journal*, April 1, May 1, 14, June 9, August 29, 1864.

2. Colonel Robert Ould, Commissioner for the Exchange of Prisoners.

3. Amelia Gorgas to Millie Crawford, Sunday, September 26, 1864, GGC.

4. Gorgas, *Journal*, November 3, 1864, GGC.

5. General Gracie was a Mobile merchant before the Civil War.

6. Amelia Gorgas to Sarah Crawford, Sunday, December 4, 1864, GGC.

7. Gorgas, *Journal*, January 4, 6, 18, 25, 1865.

8. Official Records of the Union and Confederate Armies, Series I, Vol. XLVII, Part II, 661–62.

9. Gorgas, *Journal*, March 11, 1865.

10. The note to General Ord endorsed with instructions to place a guard at Mrs. Gorgas's home is in the Gayle-Gorgas Collection.

11. Pearl's mother was Mrs. Julia Gardiner Tyler, widow of President Tyler, who corresponded with Richard Gayle during his imprisonment at Fort Warren from her family home in New York. See *Tyler's Quarterly Magazine of History and Genealogy*, XXX, 86–114, 184–207.

12. Amelia Gorgas to Richard Gayle, April 21 [1865], GGC.

13. Amelia Gorgas wrote an article, "The Evacuation of Richmond," about 1900 in which she tells this story. Tait Collection.

Chapter 10

1. Amelia Gorgas to Sarah Crawford, May 2, 1865, GGC.
2. Gorgas, *Journal*, May 4, 1865.
3. Josiah Gorgas to Amelia Gorgas, June 4, 14, 1865, GGC.
4. Amelia Gorgas to Josiah Gorgas, June 26, part of another letter, June, July 29, 1865 (Cambridge, Md.), Josiah Gorgas to Amelia Gorgas, July 19, September 11, 29, 1865, GGC.
5. Gorgas, *Journal*, October 15, 1865, November 4, December 27, 1865.
6. President Andrew Johnson.
7. Josiah Gorgas to Amelia Gorgas, January 1, 1866, Amelia Gorgas to Josiah Gorgas, December 30, 1865, GGC.
8. Gorgas, *Journal*, January 20, February 1, 1866; Amelia Gorgas to Josiah Gorgas, January 23, 1866, Josiah Gorgas to Amelia Gorgas, January 23, February 11, 1866, GGC.
9. Henry Tutwiler conducted the Greene Springs School near Havana, Alabama.
10. Josiah Gorgas to Amelia Gorgas, February 11, 1866, Amelia Gorgas to Josiah Gorgas, February 18, 1866, GGC.
11. Captain William M. Polk, son of Bishop Leonidas Polk, studied at the Virginia Military Institute.
12. Manuscript autobiographical sketch (1900), Alderman Library, University of Virginia, Charlottesville, Virginia.
13. Gorgas, *Journal*, May 3, 1866.
14. Millie Crawford is quoted in a letter from Clara Crawford to their sister Sallie Crawford, December 8, 1866, Hughes Collection.
15. Gorgas, *Journal*, January 27, 1867.
16. Ibid., June 30, August 4, 1867.
17. Clara Gayle had had a good education for her time. She spent two years studying in New York before her marriage to John Gayle.
18. Gorgas, *Journal*, December 14, 22, 1867, March 30, 1868.
19. Edmund Dargan Gayle, Amelia's half-brother.
20. Dowski McMain, son of Captain McMain, one of General Gorgas's assistants.
21. Amelia Gorgas to Willie Gorgas, Brierfield [May 1868], GGC.

Chapter 11

1. Gorgas, *Journal*, June 7, 28, 1868.
2. George R. Fairbanks, *History of the University of the South* (Jacksonville, Florida: H. & W. B. Drew Co., 1905), 35, 72, 84–85.

3. Arthur Benjamin Chitty, Jr., *Reconstruction At Sewanee* (Sewanee, Tennessee: The University Press, 1954), 102, 125.

4. Gorgas, *Journal,* October 22, 1868.

5. Amelia Gorgas to Josiah Gorgas, no date [probably summer 1869], Josiah Gorgas to Amelia Gorgas, 12 M—Monday [July 1869], Sunday, 1869 [probably mid-August], GGC.

6. Amelia Gorgas to Josiah Gorgas, August 4, 1869, Wednesday night [1869], GGC.

7. The Reverend Mr. Toomer Porter had known the Gorgas family in Charleston before the war and started a boys' school there after the war.

8. Josiah Gorgas to Amelia Gorgas, August 9, 30, October 10, 1869, GGC.

9. Ibid., Wednesday, 1869 [August].

10. Amelia Gorgas to Josiah Gorgas, October 14, 1869, GGC.

11. Josiah Gorgas to Jessie Gorgas, November 9, 1869, GGC.

12. Josiah Gorgas to Amelia Gorgas, March 6, 19, Sunday evening, 1870 [late March], GGC.

13. Amelia Gorgas to Josiah Gorgas, April 3, 1870, Wednesday night [1870], April 3 [1870], GGC.

14. Elyton later became Birmingham, Alabama.

15. Amelia Gorgas to Josiah Gorgas, Wednesday night [1870]; Thursday morning, June 2nd [1870], GGC.

Chapter 12

1. Gorgas, *Journal,* January 17, 1871.

2. Chitty, *Reconstruction at Sewanee,* 135.

3. Gorgas, *Journal,* March 3, 1872.

4. Josiah Gorgas to Amelia Gorgas, January 25, February 6, 1872, GGC.

5. The Sewanee coal train connected with the main line of the Nashville and Chattanooga Railroad at Cowan, five miles from Sewanee. Chitty, *Reconstruction at Sewanee,* 54, 159.

6. Amelia Gorgas to Jessie Gorgas, Friday [1872], GGC.

7. Amelia Gorgas to Jessie and Mamie Gorgas, June 8 [1872], GGC.

8. Fairbanks, *University of the South,* 147–48.

9. Gorgas, *Journal,* October 18, 1872.

10. Guerry, *Men Who Made Sewanee,* 73–86.

11. Amelia Gorgas to Josiah Gorgas, Monday morning [February 1873], Tait Collection.

12. Amelia Gorgas to Josiah Gorgas, Tuesday morning [February 1873], Thursday [February 1873], GGC.

13. *Sewanee* (Reprinted as *Purple Sewanee*), ed. Lily Baker, Charlotte Gailor, Rose D. Lovell, Sarah H. Torian (Sewanee, Tennessee: Association for the Preservation of Tennessee Antiquities, 1958), 45.

14. *The Sewanee Purple*, Sewanee, Tennessee, December 13, 1933. Letter from Paul McCombs, a student at Sewanee in 1874 and 1875.

15. *Purple Sewanee*, 55. See also Day Book of Miss Carrie Aiken, Gayle-Aiken Collection, South Caroliniana Library.

16. Fairbanks, *University of the South*, 177.

17. Gorgas, *Journal*, October 13, 1875.

18. Josiah Gorgas to Amelia Gorgas, January 25, 1876, GGC.

19. Dr. James Fountain Heustis, son of Dr. Jabez Heustis and Swepstone Gayle Heustis.

20. Josiah Gorgas to Amelia Gorgas, Wednesday morning [February 1876], Amelia Gorgas to W. C. Gorgas, October 14, 1877, GGC.

21. Amelia Gorgas to W. C. Gorgas, Friday night [December 1876], Sunday, December 2nd [1877], May 12, 1878, GGC.

22. Amelia Gorgas to W. C. Gorgas, Friday night [December 1876], Josiah Gorgas to W. C. Gorgas, February 21, 1877, GGC.

23. Fairbanks, *University of the South*, 174–75. On p. 177 Fairbanks calls it "a rather shabby action of the board in view of the fact that it had elected Gorgas for a term of five years only two years before."

24. Amelia Gorgas to W. C. Gorgas, October 14, 1877, Sunday, December 2nd [1877], GGC.

25. Minnie Gorgas to Jessie Gorgas, January 11, 14, 1878, Tait Collection.

26. Josiah Gorgas to Amelia Gorgas, Tuesday 5 p.m. [February 1878], Saturday 4 p.m. 1878, February 25, 1878, GGC.

27. Amelia Gorgas to W. C. Gorgas, May 12, 1878, GGC.

28. Col. H. N. R. Dawson of Selma, Alabama.

29. Josiah Gorgas to W. C. Gorgas, July 8, 1878, GGC.

Chapter 13

1. Josiah Gorgas to W. M. Green, July 27, 1878, Proceedings of the Board of Trustees, University of the South, 1878, 10–11.

2. Mary Gayle Aiken to "My dear Sister," July 28, 1878, Gorgas Papers, Jessie Ball duPont Library, University of the South.

3. Josiah Gorgas to Amelia Gorgas, August 29, 1878, GGC.

4. *Catalogue of the Officers and Students of the University of Alabama, Session of 1878–79*, Tuscaloosa, Alabama, 1879.

5. Josiah Gorgas to Amelia Gorgas, September 16, 19, December 2, 1878, GGC.

6. Clara Crawford, Sarah's oldest daughter died in 1875. Sarah's son had moved to Texas.

7. Josiah Gorgas to Amelia Gorgas, October 31, 1878, GGC.

8. William M. Green to Amelia Gorgas, December 23, 1878, GGC.

9. Josiah Gorgas to Amelia Gorgas, December 24, 1878, Amelia Gorgas to W. C. Gorgas, January 16 [1879], GGC.

10. T. C. McCorvey to Netta Tutwiler, January 18, 1879. Letter in possession of G. B. Johnston, Blacksburg, Virginia. Miss Tutwiler, daughter of Henry Tutwiler of Greene Springs School, married T. C. McCorvey July 22, 1880, and became one of Amelia Gorgas's campus friends.

11. Josiah Gorgas to Amelia Gorgas, February 20, 22, 1879, GGC.

12. Dr. James T. Searcy succeeded Dr. Bryce as head of the Alabama Insane Hospital in 1892.

13. Amelia Gorgas to W. C. Gorgas, March 8, 1879, Thomas L. Bayne to Amelia Gorgas, February 28, 1879, GGC.

14. Mary Aiken to Maria Bayne, March 19, 1879, GGC.

15. Amelia Gorgas to W. C. Gorgas, October 2, 1879, GGC.

16. *Montgomery Advertiser and Mail*, December 28, 1879.

17. Amelia Gorgas to Thomas L. Bayne, January 12, 1881, GGC.

18. W. C. Gorgas to Jessie Gorgas, February 27, 1882, GGC.

19. Amelia Gorgas to Sarah Crawford, May 17, 1883, GGC.

20. William P. DuBose to Amelia Gorgas, May 25, 1883, GGC. The Reverend Mr. DuBose's first wife was the former Nannie Peronneau.

21. Burwell Boykin Lewis to Amelia Gorgas, July 14, 1883, GGC.

22. This draft is written on the back of President Lewis's letter to Mrs. Gorgas.

23. Minute on the Death of General Josiah Gorgas, June 18, 1883. Newspaper copy in Amelia Gorgas Scrapbook, Tait Collection.

24. Amelia Gorgas to Thomas Bayne, November 1, 1883, GGC.

Chapter 14

1. Amelia Gorgas to Thomas L. Bayne, July 24, 1883, GGC.

2. Thomas L. Bayne's "Sketch of the Life of Josiah Gorgas" was published in the *Southern Historical Papers*, XIII (1885), 216–28.

3. Amelia Gorgas to Thomas L. Bayne, August 9, November 1, 1883, GGC.

4. Amelia Gorgas to W. C. Gorgas, April 6, 1884, GGC.

5. Extract from address of B. B. Lewis, May 5, 1884. Copied in longhand in Amelia Gayle Gorgas Scrapbook.

6. Gorgas and Hendrick, *William Crawford Gorgas*, 6–10.

7. Amelia Gorgas to W. C. Gorgas, August 6, 1884.

8. Gorgas and Hendrick, *William Crawford Gorgas*, 17–18.

9. New Orleans *Times-Democrat*, September 20, October 2, 1885.

10. Amelia Gorgas to W. C. Gorgas, October 4, 1886, GGC.

11. J. W. Mallet to Amelia Gorgas, March 1, 1887, GGC. Story recalled by Minnie Gorgas Palfrey, Tait Collection.

12. Amelia Gorgas to Mamie Gorgas, Sunday morning [June 1888], Tait Collection. Amelia Gorgas to W. C. Gorgas, part of a letter [June or July 1888] GGC.

13. New Orleans *Times-Democrat*, June 23, 1888.

14. *Annual Report of the President of the University of Alabama*, 1891–1892.

15. Maria Gorgas to Amelia Gorgas, May 27 [1892], Amelia Gorgas to Maria Gorgas, May 10, 1894, Tait Collection.

16. Maria Gorgas to Amelia Gorgas, part of a letter [June 1898], GGC.

17. New Orleans *Times-Democrat*, February 9, 1895.

18. Amelia Gorgas to Maria Gorgas, May 10, 1894, Tait Collection; Amelia Gorgas to Maria Gorgas, February 9, 1896, GGC.

19. *Atlanta Constitution*, Sunday, June 16, 1895.

20. *Corolla* owned by Miss Mary Hughes.

21. Jessie Gorgas to W. C. Gorgas, October 3, 1894, Manuscripts Division, Library of Congress; Amelia Gorgas to Maria Gorgas, October 20, 1894, Tait Collection.

22. Amelia Gorgas to Marie Gorgas, October 24, 1894, Library of Congress.

23. Amelia Gorgas to W. C. Gorgas, May 25, 1898, Library of Congress. Bishop Gailor succeeded Bishop Quintard as Bishop of Tennessee.

24. Amelia Gorgas to W. C. Gorgas, October 3, 1898, GGC.

25. Women were first admitted to The University of Alabama in 1893.

26. Amelia Gorgas to W. C. Gorgas, June 16, 1899, Library of Congress.

Chapter 15

1. John Mendinghall Gibson, *Physician to the World: The Life of General William C. Gorgas* (Durham, North Carolina: Duke University Press, 1950), 56–90.

2. Amelia Gorgas to W. C. Gorgas, July 1900, GGC.

3. Amelia Gorgas to W. C. Gorgas, February 12, 1901, July 3, 1901, Library of Congress.

4. John H. Bankhead was congressman from Alabama—later senator.

5. W. C. Gorgas to Amelia Gorgas, March 7, 1903, GGC.

6. Amelia Gorgas to W. C. Gorgas, July 3, 1901, Library of Congress.

7. Amelia Gorgas to Maria Gorgas, August 4, 1903, GGC.

8. Amelia Gorgas to Maria Gorgas, September 1, 1903, Tait Collection.

9. W. C. Gorgas to Maria Gorgas, August 15, 1904, GGC. Gibson, *Physician to the World*, gives a fascinating and detailed account of this work.

10. Amelia Gorgas to Minnie Palfrey, May 4, 1904, Amelia Gorgas to Maria Gorgas, August 2, 1904, Tait Collection.

11. Tuscaloosa *Times Gazette*, May 30, 1905.

12. Clipping in Amelia Gayle Gorgas Scrapbook, Tait Collection.

13. Amelia Gorgas to Minnie Palfrey, Tuesday, June 1906, Tait Collection; Amelia Gorgas to Marie Gorgas, July 24, 1906, GGC. Mary Aiken died in 1911.

14. Letter from President Henry S. Pritchett, President of the Carnegie Foundation, December 18, 1906, GGC.

15. W. C. Gorgas to Amelia Gorgas, October 17, 1905, GGC.

16. Gibson, *Physician to the World*, 176–77.

17. W. C. Gorgas to Amelia Gorgas, October 11, 1912, GGC.

18. Quoted by Amelia Gayle Gorgas's granddaughter, Tait Collection.

BIBLIOGRAPHY

Alabama Portraits Prior to 1870. National Society of the Colonial Dames of America in the State of Alabama. Mobile, Alabama: Gill Printing and Stationery Co., 1969.

Alabama University Monthly. Tuscaloosa, Alabama, 1877, 1878. Volumes V and VI.

Boatner, Mark Mayo, III. *The Civil War Dictionary*. New York: David McKay Co., 1959.

Brewer, Willis. *Alabama: Her History, Resources, War Record, and Public Men From 1540 to 1872*. Montgomery, Alabama: Barrett and Brown, 1872.

Chesnut, Mary Boykin. *A Diary from Dixie*. Boston: Houghton Mifflin Co., 1949.

Chitty, Arthur Benjamin, Jr. *Reconstruction at Sewanee*. Sewanee, Tennessee: The University Press, 1954.

Clinton, Matthew William. *Tuscaloosa, Alabama, Its Early Days*. Tuscaloosa, Alabama: The Zonta Club, 1958.

Clay-Clopton, Virginia. *A Belle of the Fifties. Memoirs of Mrs. Clay of Alabama—Put Into Narrative Form by Ada Sterling*. New York: Doubleday, Page and Co., 1905.

Coit, Margaret L. *John C. Calhoun, American Patriot*. Boston: Houghton Mifflin Co., 1950.

Cole, Arthur Charles. *The Whig Party in the South*. Gloucester, Massachusetts: Peter Smith, 1962.

Connor, Henry G. *John Archibald Campbell*. Boston and New York: Houghton Mifflin Co., 1920.

Congressional Globe. Washington: Blair and Rives, 1848.

Corolla 1893, 1896, 1897, 1898, 1899, 1905, 1906. Published by the Students of the University of Alabama.

Craighead, Edwin S., and Craighead, Frank. *Craighead's Mobile*, ed. Caldwell Delaney. Mobile, Alabama: The Haunted Bookshop, 1968.

Current, Richard N., Williams, T. Harry, and Freidel, Frank. *American History: A Survey*. New York: Alfred A. Knopf, 1961.

De Leon, Thomas Cooper. *Belles, Beaux and Brains of the 60's*. New York: G. W. Dillingham Co., 1909.

————. *Four Years in Rebel Capitals*. Mobile, Alabama: The Gossip Printing Co., 1890.

Fairbanks, George R. *History of the University of the South.* Jacksonville, Florida: H & W. B. Drew Co., 1905.

Fidler, William Perry. *Augusta Evans Wilson, 1835–1909: A Biography.* University, Alabama: University of Alabama Press, 1951.

Fry, Anna M. Gayle. *Memories of Old Cahaba.* Nashville, Tennessee and Dallas, Texas: Publishing House of the M. E. Church, 1908. (Reprinted by the Strode Publishers, Huntsville, Alabama, 1972.)

Garrett, William. *Reminiscences of Public Men in Alabama for Thirty Years.* Atlanta, Georgia: Plantation Publishing Company's Press, 1872.

Gayle, Sarah Haynesworth. *Extracts from the Journal of Sarah Haynesworth Gayle.* (Selected and published by one of her grandchildren, Edith Bayne Denegre.) New Rochelle, New York: The Knickerbocker Press, 1895.

Gibson, John Mendinghall. *Physician to the World: The Life of General William C. Gorgas.* Durham, North Carolina: Duke University Press, 1950.

Gilmer, George R. *Sketches of Some of the First Settlers of Upper Georgia, of the Cherokees, and the Author.* Americus, Georgia: Americus Book Co., 1926.

Gorgas, Marie D., and Hendrick, Burton J. *William Crawford Gorgas, His Life and Work.* Garden City, New York: Doubleday, Page and Co., 1924.

Guerry, Moultrie. *Men Who Made Sewanee.* Sewanee, Tennessee: The University Press, 1932.

Hamilton, Holman. *Zachary Taylor: Soldier in the White House.* Indianapolis and New York: Bobbs-Merrill Co., 1951.

Harrison, Mrs. Burton. *Recollections Grave and Gay.* New York: Charles Scribner's Sons, 1911.

Haynsworth, Hugh C. *Haynsworth-Furman and Allied Families.* Sumter, South Carolina, 1942.

Hollis, Christopher. *The American Heresy.* New York: Minton, Balch & Co., 1930.

Hughes, Nathaniel Cheairs, Jr. *General William J. Hardee: Old Reliable.* Baton Rouge, Louisiana: Louisiana State University Press, 1965.

Jones, John Beauchamp. *A Rebel War Clerk's Diary.* Condensed, edited, and annotated by Earl Schenk Miers. New York: Sagamore Press, 1958.

Jones, Katherine M. *Heroines of Dixie.* Indianapolis and New York: Bobbs-Merrill Co., 1955.

——. *Ladies of Richmond, Confederate Capital.* Indianapolis and New York: Bobbs-Merrill Co., 1962.

Kean, Robert Garlick Hill. *Inside the Confederate Government: The Diary of Robert Garlick Hill Kean.* ed. Edward Younger. New York: Oxford University Press, 1957.

Kimmel, Stanley Preston. *Mr. Davis's Richmond.* New York: Bramhall House, 1958.

Leach, Joseph. *Bright Particular Star: The Life and Times of Charlotte Cushman*. New Haven and London: Yale University Press, 1970.

McCorvey, Thomas Chalmers. *Alabama Historical Sketches*. Charlottesville, Virginia: University of Virginia Press, 1960.

McMillan, Malcolm Cook. *The Alabama Confederate Reader*. University, Alabama: University of Alabama Press, 1963.

Maury, Dabney H. *Recollections of a Virginian*. New York: Charles Scribner's Sons, 1894.

Maury, Sarah Mytton. *Statesmen of America in 1846*. Philadelphia: Carey and Hart, 1847.

Merrill, Eleanor Brown. *A Virginia Heritage*. Richmond, Virginia: Whittet and Shepperson, 1968.

Moore, Albert Burton. *History of Alabama and Her People*, 3 vols. Chicago and New York: The American Historical Society, 1927.

Munford, Robert Beverley, Jr. *Richmond Homes and Memories*. Richmond, Virginia: Garrett and Massie, 1936.

Owen, Thomas McAdory. "A Bibliography of Alabama," *Annual Report of the American Historical Association for the Year 1897*. Washington, D.C.: Government Printing Office, 1898.

————. *History of Alabama and Dictionary of Alabama Biography*, 4 vols. Chicago: The S. J. Clarke Publishing Co., 1921.

Palmer, Thomas Waverly. *A Register of the Officers and Students of the University of Alabama 1831–1901*. Tuscaloosa, Alabama: University of Alabama, 1901.

Parks, Joseph Howard. *General Edmund Kirby Smith, C.S.A.* Baton Rouge, Louisiana: Louisiana State University Press, 1954.

Percy, William Alexander. *Lanterns on the Levee*. New York: Alfred A. Knopf, 1941.

Pickett, Albert James. *The History of Alabama and Incidentally of Georgia and Mississippi, From the Earliest Period*. Sheffield, Alabama: Robert C. Randolph, 1896.

————and Owen, Thomas McAdory. *Annals of Alabama*, 1819–1900 (included as an appendix to Pickett). Birmingham, Alabama, 1900.

Polk, William Mecklenburg. *Leonidas Polk: Bishop and General*, 2 vols. New York: Longmans, Green and Co., 1915.

Putnam, Sallie A. *In Richmond During the Confederacy by A Lady of Richmond*. New York: Robert M. McBride Co., 1961. Reprinted from the 1867 edition.

Ross, Ishbel. *First Lady of the South: The Life of Mrs. Jefferson Davis*. New York: Harper and Brothers, 1958.

Royall, Anne Newport. *Letters from Alabama 1817–1822*. Biographical Introduction and Notes by Lucille Griffith. University, Alabama: University of Alabama Press, 1969.

Scott, Mary Wingfield. *Houses of Old Richmond.* New York: Bonanza Books, 1941.

———. *Old Richmond Neighborhoods.* Richmond, Virginia: Whittet and Shepperson, 1950.

Sellers, James B. *History of the University of Alabama 1818-1902,* Vol. I. University, Alabama: University of Alabama Press, 1953.

Sewanee (Reprinted as *Purple Sewanee*). Eds. Lily Baker, Charlotte Gailor, Rose Duncan Lovell, Sarah Hodgson Torian. Sewanee, Tennessee: Association for the Preservation of Tennessee Antiquities, 1961.

Shackelford, George Green, ed. *Collected Papers to Commemorate Fifty Years of the Monticello Association of the Descendants of Thomas Jefferson.* Princeton: The Monticello Association, 1965.

Smedes, Susan Dabney. *Memorials of a Southern Planter.* Baltimore: Cushing and Bailey, 1888.

Smith, William R., Sr. *Reminiscences of a Long Life,* Vol. I. Washington, D.C., 1889.

Stanard, Mary Newton. *Richmond: Its People and Its Story.* Philadelphia and London: J. B. Lippincott Co., 1923.

Strode, Hudson. *Jefferson Davis,* 3 vols. New York: Harcourt, Brace and World, 1955-1964.

Sulzby, James F., Jr. *Historic Alabama Hotels and Resorts.* University, Alabama: University of Alabama Press, 1960.

Summersell, Charles Grayson. *Historical Foundations of Mobile.* University, Alabama: University of Alabama Press, 1949.

Thomas, Emory M. *The Confederate State of Richmond: A Biography of the Capital.* Austin and London: University of Texas Press, 1971.

University of Alabama Bulletin: Seventy-Fifth Anniversary Commemoration Number. New Series, November 1906 (Number 3).

Vandiver, Frank E. *Ploughshares Into Swords: Josiah Gorgas and Confederate Ordnance.* Austin: University of Texas Press, 1952.

———, ed. *The Civil War Diary of General Josiah Gorgas.* University, Alabama: University of Alabama Press, 1947.

Verner, Clara L. *Amelia Gayle Gorgas: A Sketch.* Montgomery, Alabama: The Paragon Press, 1937.

Warner, Ezra J. *Generals in Gray.* Baton Rouge, Louisiana: Louisiana State University Press, 1959.

Wilmer, Richard Hooker. *The Recent Past from a Southern Standpoint.* New York: Thomas Whittaker, 1887.

Wright, Mrs. D. Giraud (Louise Wigfall). *A Southern Girl in '61.* New York: Doubleday, Page and Co., 1905.

Yerby, William E. W. *History of Greensboro, Alabama From Its Earliest Settlement.* Montgomery, Alabama: The Paragon Press, 1908.

Young, James Sterling. *The Washington Community 1800–1828.* New York and London: Columbia University Press, 1966.

Wiltse, Charles Maurice. *John C. Calhoun, Sectionalist 1840–1850.* Indianapolis and New York: Bobbs-Merrill Co., 1951.

Manuscripts

Bayne-Gayle Papers, Southern Historical Collection, University of North Carolina Library, Chapel Hill, North Carolina.

Gayle-Aiken Papers, South Caroliniana Library, University of South Carolina, Columbia, South Carolina.

Gayle-Gorgas Collection, Amelia Gayle Gorgas Library, University of Alabama, University, Alabama.

Papers of William Crawford Gorgas, Manuscript Collection, Library of Congress.

Papers of Mary Adams Hughes, Edgefield, South Carolina.

Papers of Thomas Chalmers McCorvey, George Burke Johnston, Blacksburg, Virginia.

Papers of George Tait, Richmond, Virginia.

Mallet Papers, Alderman Library, University of Virginia, Charlottesville, Virginia.

Gorgas Papers, Jessie Ball duPont Library, University of the South, Sewanee, Tennessee.

INDEX

Amelia Gayle Gorgas: A Bibliography
was composed in VIP Janson by
The Composing Room of Grand Rapids, Michigan.
Printed by McNaughton-Gunn, Inc. Ann Arbor, Michigan.
Bound by John H. Dekker and Sons Grand Rapids, Michigan.
Endsheet illustration courtesy of the
First Alabama Bank of Tuscaloosa, N.A.
Book design by Anna Fleck Jacobs.
Production supervision: Paul R. Kennedy.